The Encyclopedia of
PICTURE CHORDS
for Guitar & Keyboard

compiled by Len Vogler

Guarantees that you will never be at a loss for the right chord! Complete with special sections on scales, intervals, and chord construction; progressions; moveable chords; alternate chord names; and much more.

Amsco Publications
New York/London/Sydney

W9-BYO-349

Cover photography by Randall Wallace
Interior design and layout by Len Vogler

Order No. AM 945285
US International Standard Book Number: 0.8256.1638.7
UK International Standard Book Number: 0.7119.6749.0

Exclusive Distributors:
Music Sales Corporation
257 Park Avenue South, New York, NY 10010 USA
Music Sales Limited
8/9 Frith Street, London W1V 5TZ England
Music Sales Pty. Limited
120 Rothschild Street, Rosebery, Sydney, NSW 2018, Australia

Printed in the United States of America by
Vicks Lithograph and Printing Corporation

Contents

Chord Construction

Scales

In order to talk about chord structure we need to discuss the foundation by which chords are formed—*scales*. There are a multitude of scales available to the musician, but we will explain only those that are most pertinent—the major, minor, and chromatic scales.

Major

Natural minor

Harmonic minor

Melodic minor

Chromatic

Scales are determined by the distribution of *half steps* and *whole steps*. For example, the major scale has half steps between scale steps three and four, and between seven and eight. The harmonic minor has half steps between scale steps two and three, five and six, and seven and eight. The melodic minor scale's ascending order finds half steps between scale steps two and three, and between seven and eight. Descending, the half steps fall between scale steps six and five, and between three and two; and a whole step is now in place between eight and seven.

It is common to refer to scale steps, or *degrees,* by Roman numerals as in the example above and also by the following names:

I. Tonic
II. Supertonic
III. Mediant
IV. Subdominant
V. Dominant
VI. Submediant
VII. Leading tone

Intervals

An *interval* is the distance between two notes. This is the basis for harmony (chords). The naming of intervals, as in the example below, is fairly standard, but you may encounter other terminology in various forms of musical literature.

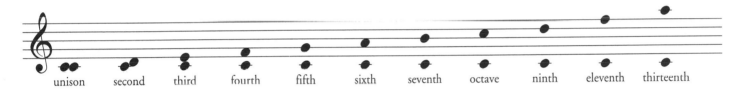

unison   second   third   fourth   fifth   sixth   seventh   octave   ninth   eleventh   thirteenth

Chords

Chords are produced by combining two or more intervals, and the simplest of these combinations is a *triad.* A triad consists of three notes obtained by the superposition of two thirds. The notes are called the *root,* the *third,* and the *fifth.*

fifth
third
root

Inversions

Inversions are produced by arranging the intervals of a chord in a different order. A triad that has the root as the bottom or lowest tone is said to be in *root position.* A triad with a third as the bottom or lowest tone is in *first inversion,* and a triad with a fifth as the bottom or lowest tone is in *second inversion.* As the chords become more complex—such as, sixths, sevenths, etc.—there will be more possible inversions.

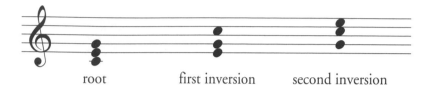

root   first inversion   second inversion

Note that when inverting more complex chords the inversion may actually become a completely different chord.

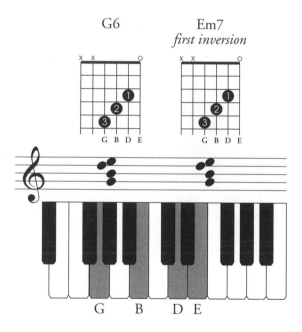

Altered Triads

When a chord consists of a root, major third, and a perfect fifth it is known as a *major triad*. When the triad is altered by lowering the major third one half-step, it becomes a *minor triad*. The examples below are chords that have altered intervals.

Enharmonic Spelling

Enharmonie tones are tones that have different notation or spelling, but have the same pitch; like C♯ and D♭. You will encounter these differences throughout this book, mostly as altered triads. The reason that this occurs is to make it easier to read while playing from a piece of music manuscript. In the following example, D♭m7♭9 demonstrates why this approach is practical and preferred. As stated before, triads are superposed thirds or notes that are stacked one on top of the other. This allows the musician to see, at a glance, what chord they are going to play. So with this in mind, look at the D♭m7♭9 example. You will notice that the E♭ is double flatted (E♭♭) this allows the musician, again at a glance, to see that what would be the nine of the chord is now flatted. The other example is indeed the same chord, but by using the D instead of the E♭♭ the chords becomes harder to read.

How to Use This Book

The Guitar Chord Diagram

The chords are displayed as diagrams that represent the fingerboard of the guitar. There are six vertical lines representing the six strings of the guitar. Horizontal lines represent the frets. The strings are arranged with the high E (first, or thinnest) string to the right, and the low E (sixth, or thickest) to the left. The black circles indicate at which fret the finger is to be placed and the number tells you which finger to use. On some of the diagrams the black circles are smaller, this represents an optional fingering. This means you have the option of playing the note or you can choose not to use that note when making up the chord. At the top of the diagram there is a thick black line indicating the nut of the guitar. Diagrams for chords up the neck just have a fret line at the top with a Roman numeral to the right to identify the first fret of the diagram. Above the chord diagram you will occasionally see x's and o's. An x indicates that the string below it is either not played or damped, an o simply means the string is played as an open string. At the bottom of the diagram are the note names that make up the chord. This information can be helpful when making up lead licks or chord solos. A curved line tells you to bar the strings with the finger shown; that is, lay your finger flat across the indicated strings.

The fingerings in this book might be different from fingerings you have encountered in other chord books. They were chosen for their overall practicality in the majority of situations.

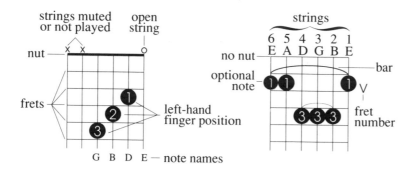

The Guitar Photo

The photo to left of each chord diagram shows you what your hand should look like on the guitar fingerboard. You will notice that the finger positions in some of the photos are a little to the right or left of the frame. This is done to show the particular chord forms proximity to either the twelfth fret or the nut of the guitar. This makes it easier to recognize the relative position on the fretboard at a glance.

Although the photos are a visual reference, all of the fingers in a given shot may not be in a proper playing position. We have sometimes moved unused fingers *out of the way*, to give you a better look at where the fretting fingers are placed. For instance, when playing the Absus4 shown in the photograph below, your second and third finger should not be tucked under the neck, they would be relaxed and extended upward over the fingerboard. Make sure your fingers are comfortable and that you are capable of moving them easily from one chord position to another.

The Keyboard Chord Diagram

The *chord name* is just that, the name of the chord. There are different names and symbols for chords, but the names used in this book are fairly common and are what you are likely to see in sheet music and music books (for alternate chord names see page 231).

The *keyboard diagram,* under the photo, shows which keys are used to make up the chord. These are the grayed areas of the diagram.

Finally, the *notes of the chord* are directly below the keyboard diagram. These are the notes that make up the chord. Sometimes you will see note names that may not be familiar to you, like C♭ or B♯. Don't panic, these are enharmonic spellings (explained on page 11).

The Keyboard Photo

The photo shows you where to put your hands on the keyboard. Most of the photos use hand positions that were chosen with the beginning player in mind—basically these fingerings are the easiest and most comfortable in most situations. You will notice that the hands are not centered on every photograph, this is to show how the hand moves in relationship to the tonic or root note and to provide you with a better viewpoint when playing these chords on your piano or electronic keyboard (your keyboard doesn't move— your hands do).

C Chords

C major

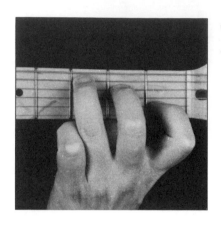 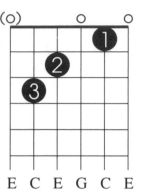

E C E G C E

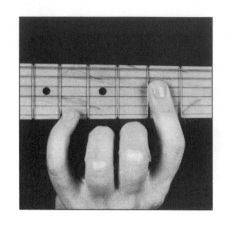 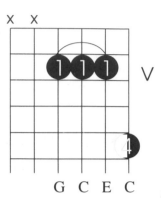

G C E C

V

Csus4

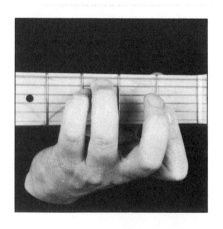 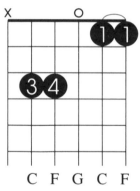

C F G C F

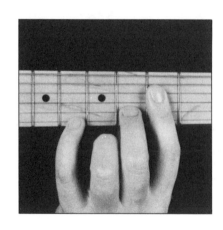 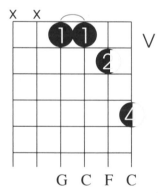

G C F C

V

C6

 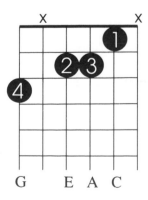

G E A C

 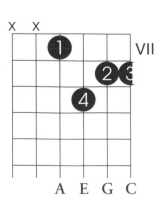

A E G C

VII

C major

C   E   G

C major *first inversion*

E   G   C

Csus4

C   F   G

Csus4 *first inversion*

F   G   C

C6

C   E   G A

C6 *first inversion*

E   G A   C

C7

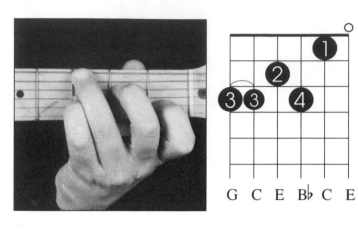

G C E B♭ C E

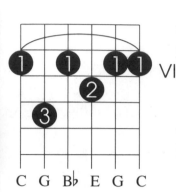

C G B♭ E G C · VII

C°7

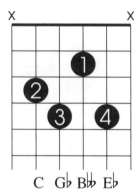

C G♭ B♭♭ E♭

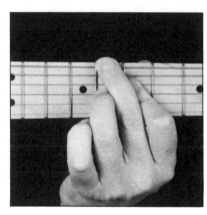

C B♭♭ E♭ G♭ · VII

C major7

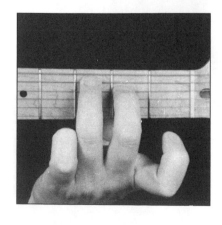

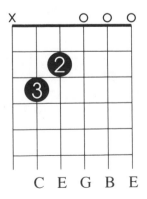

C E G B E

C E G B · VII

C7

C E G B♭

C7 *first inversion*

E G B♭ C

C°7

C E♭ G♭ B♭♭

C°7 *first inversion*

E♭ G♭ B♭♭ C

C major7

C E G B

C major7 *first inversion*

E G B C

C minor

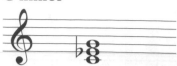

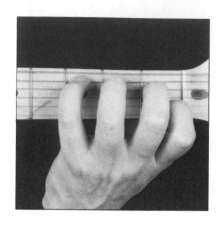

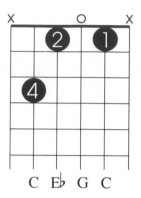

C Eb G C

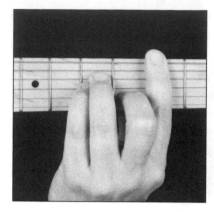

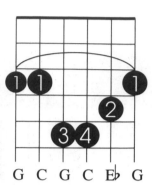

G C G C Eb G

C minor6

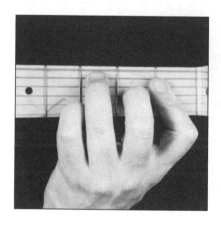

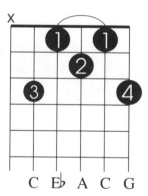

C Eb A C G

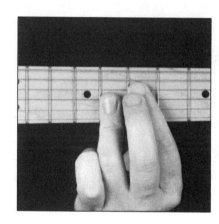

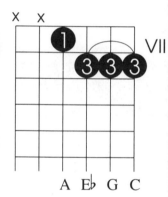

VII

A Eb G C

C minor7

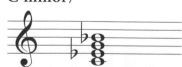

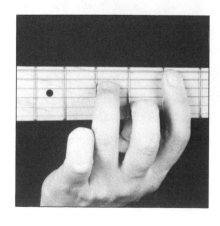

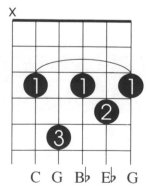

C G Bb Eb G

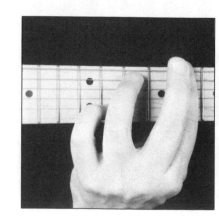

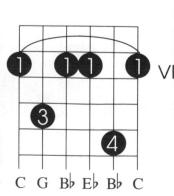

VI

C G Bb Eb Bb C

C minor

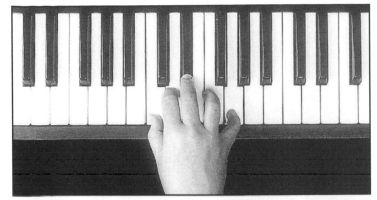

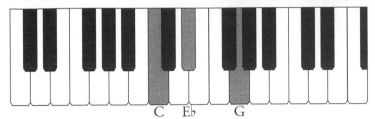

C   E♭   G

C minor *first inversion*

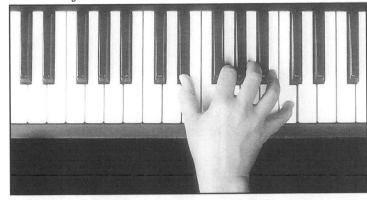

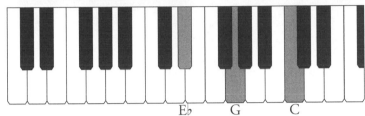

E♭   G   C

C minor6

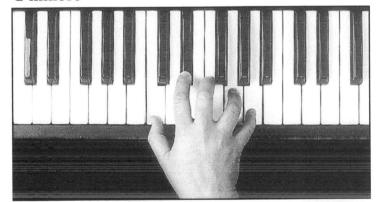

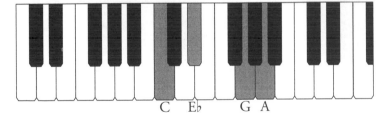

C   E♭   G   A

C minor6 *first inversion*

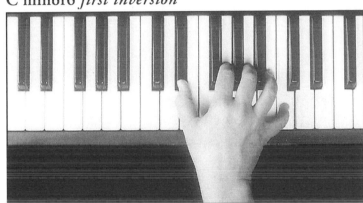

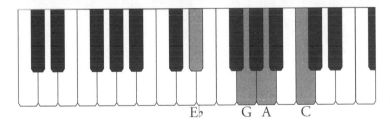

E♭   G   A   C

C minor7

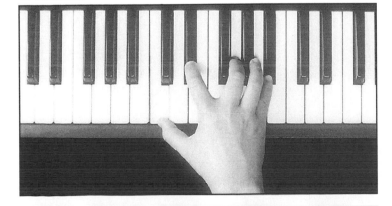

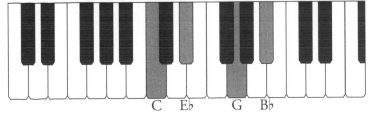

C   E♭   G   B♭

C minor7 *first inversion*

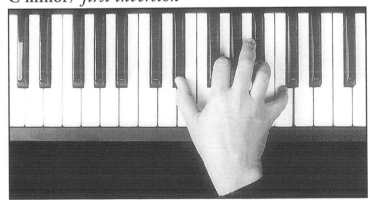

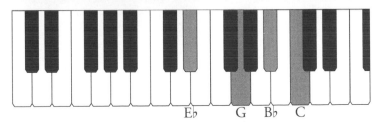

E♭   G   B♭   C

C minor7♭5

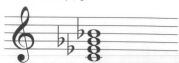

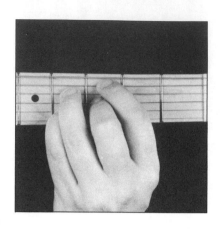

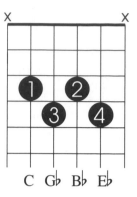

C G♭ B♭ E♭

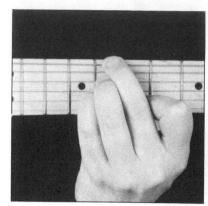

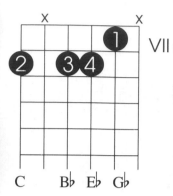

VII

C   B♭ E♭ G♭

C minor (major7)

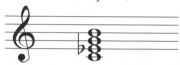

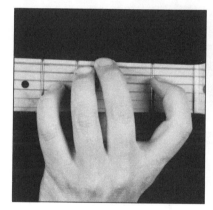

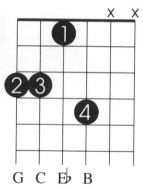

G C E♭ B

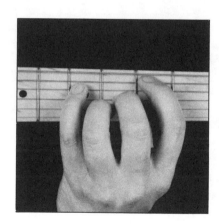

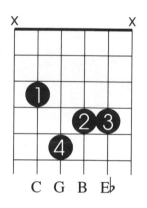

C G B E♭

C minor7♭5

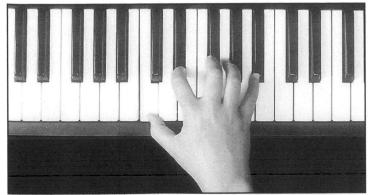

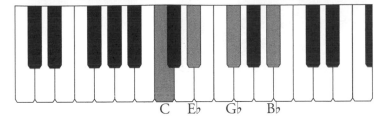

C E♭ G♭ B♭

C minor7♭5 *first inversion*

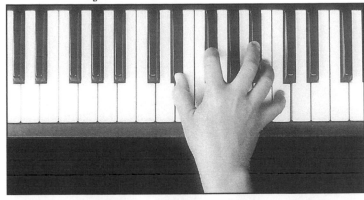

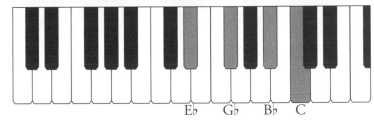

E♭ G♭ B♭ C

C minor (major7)

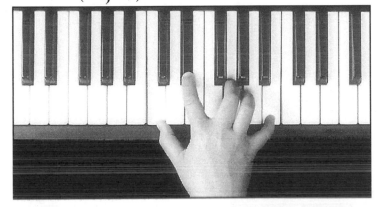

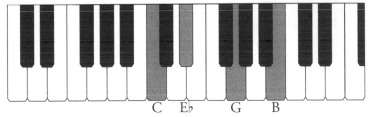

C E♭ G B

C minor (major7) *first inversion*

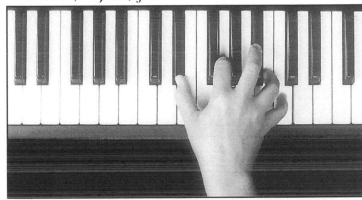

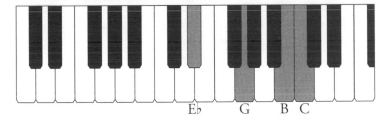

E♭ G B C

C6/9

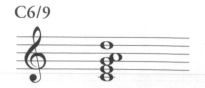

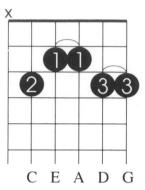

C E A D G

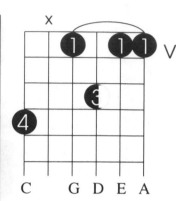

C G D E A

C9

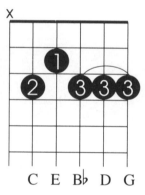

C E B♭ D G

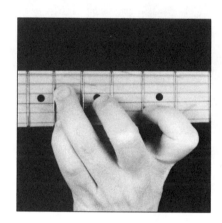

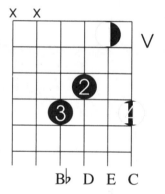

B♭ D E C

C9sus4

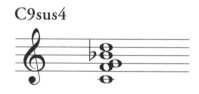

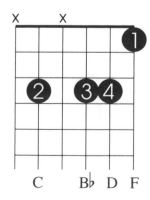

C B♭ D F

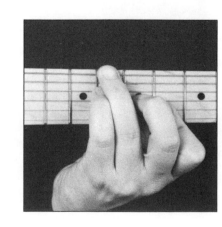

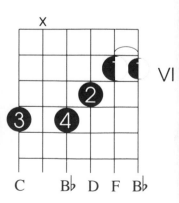

C B♭ D F B♭

C6/9

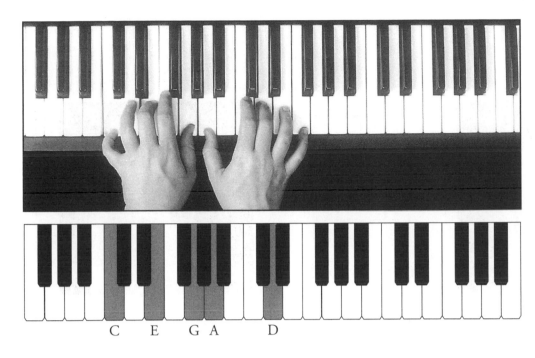

C E G A D

C9

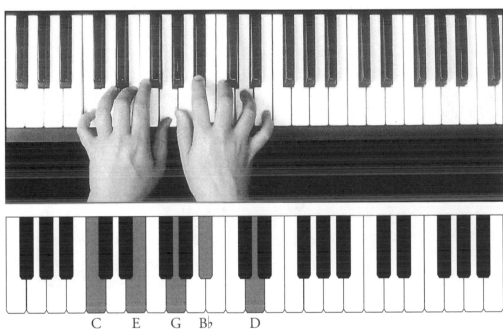

C E G B♭ D

C9sus4

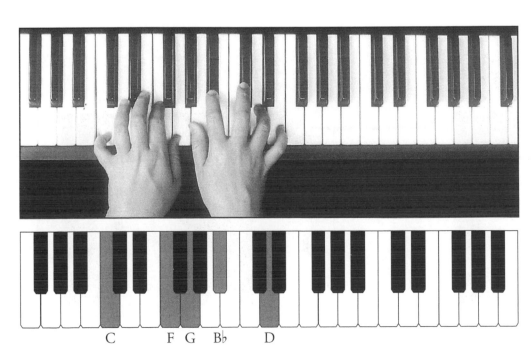

C F G B♭ D

C9♭5

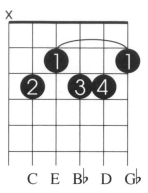

C E B♭ D G♭

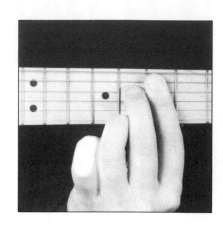

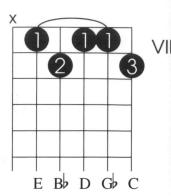

VII

E B♭ D G♭ C

C9♯5

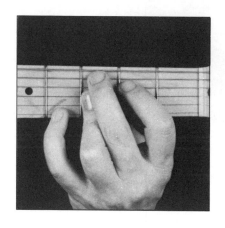

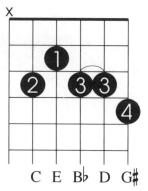

C E B♭ D G♯

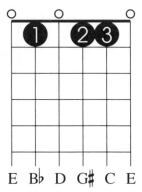

E B♭ D G♯ C E

C13

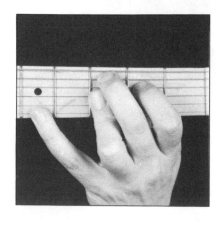

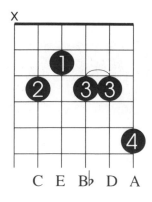

C E B♭ D A

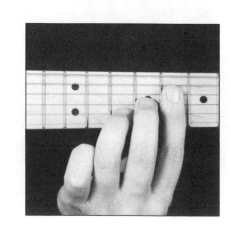

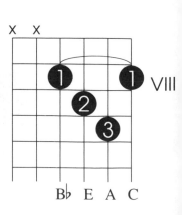

VIII

B♭ E A C

C9♭5

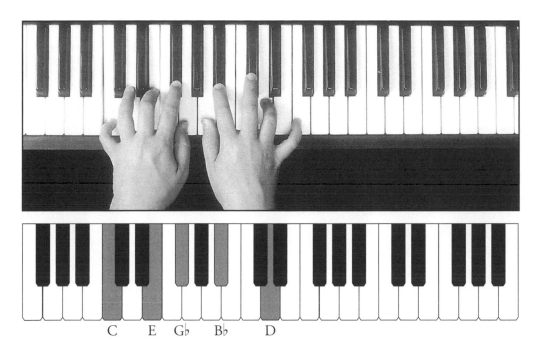

C   E   G♭   B♭   D

C9♯5

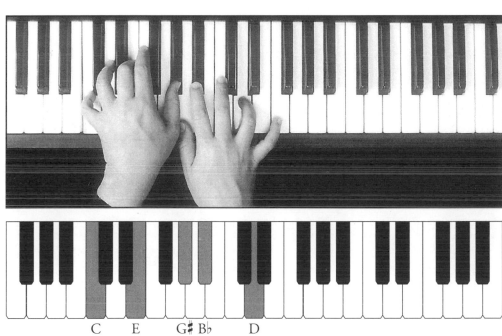

C   E   G♯ B♭   D

C13

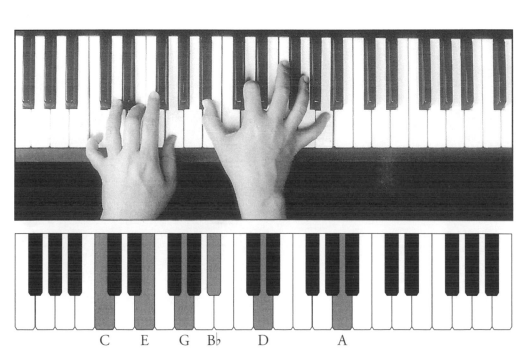

C   E   G   B♭   D   A

C major9

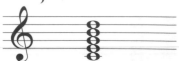

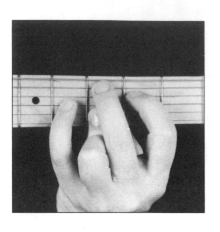

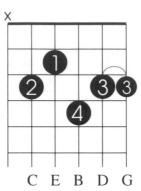

C E B D G

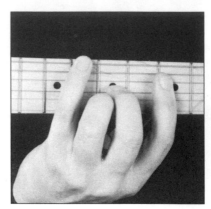

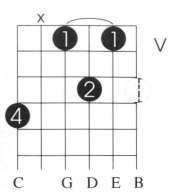

V

C G D E B

C major13

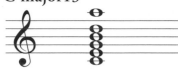

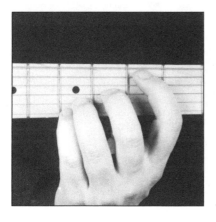

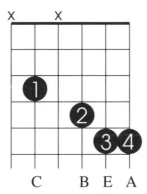

C B E A

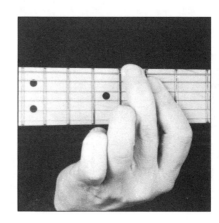

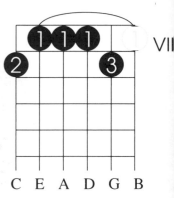

VII

C E A D G B

C minor9

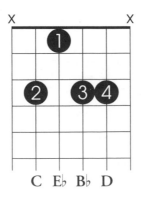

C E♭ B♭ D

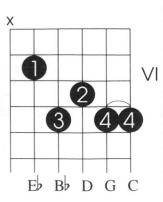

VI

E♭ B♭ D G C

C major9

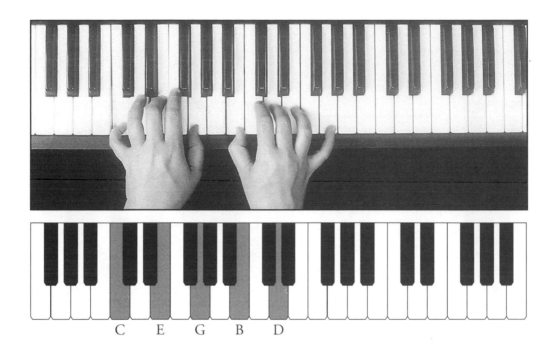

C E G B D

C major13

C E G B D A

C minor9

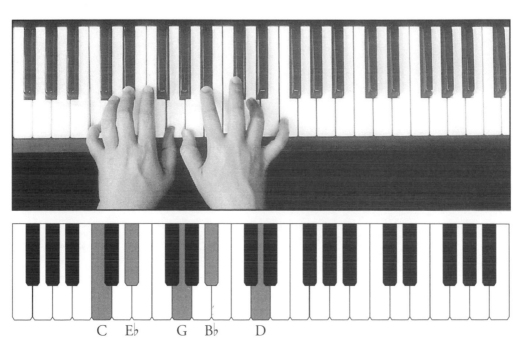

C E♭ G B♭ D

C minor11

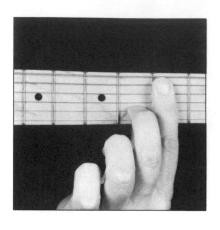

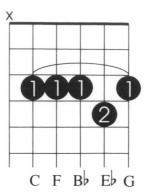

C F B♭ E♭ G

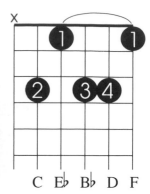

C E♭ B♭ D F

C minor13

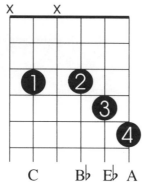

C B♭ E♭ A

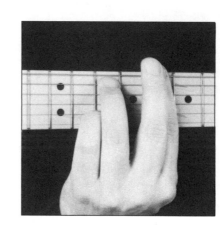

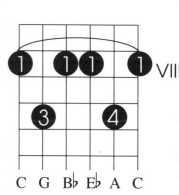

VIII

C G B♭ E♭ A C

C minor11

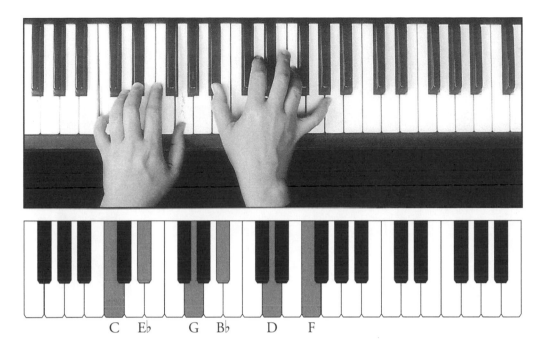

C minor13

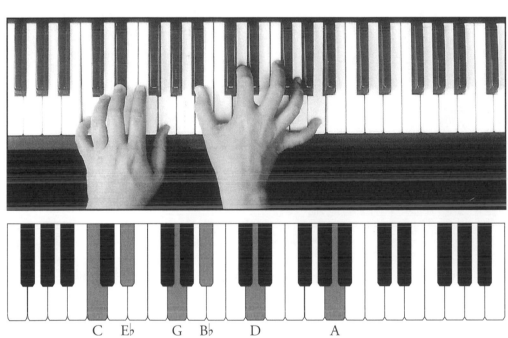

D♭/C♯ Chords

C♯ major

C♯ E♯ G♯ C♯ E♯

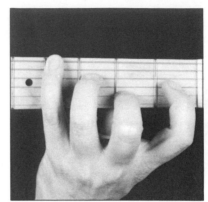

G♯ E♯ G♯ C♯

C♯sus4

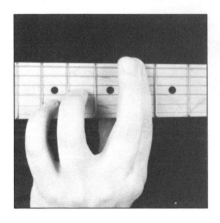

IV

G♯ C♯ F♯ C♯ F♯ G♯

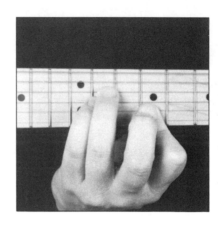

IX

C♯ F♯ G♯ C♯

C♯6

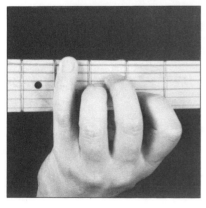

G♯ E♯ A♯ C♯

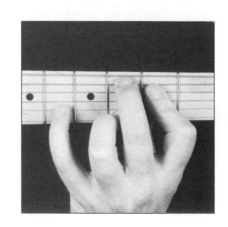

III

C♯ E♯ A♯ E♯ G♯

30

Db major

Db major *first inversion*

Dbsus4

Dbsus4 *first inversion*

Db6

Db6 *first inversion*

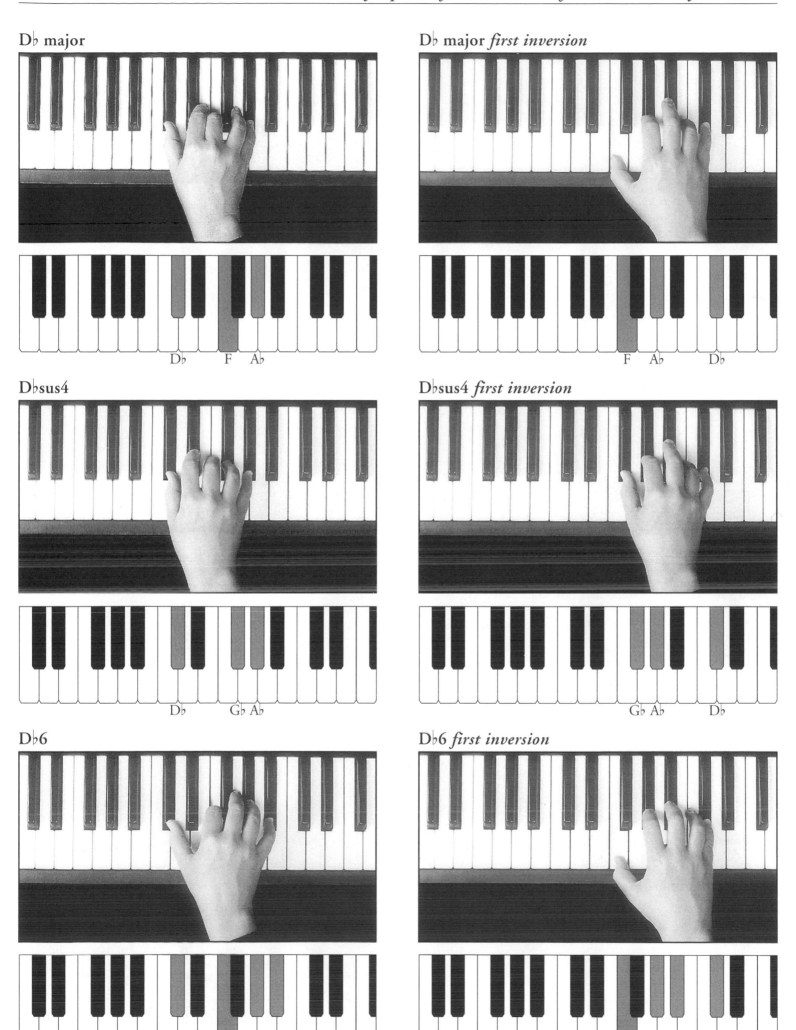

C#7

G# C# E# B C#

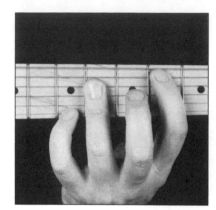

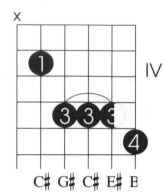

IV

C# G# C# E# B

C#°7

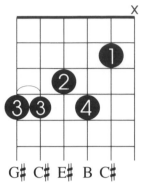

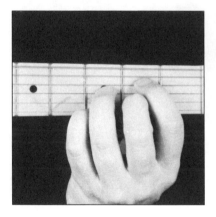

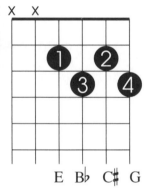

E Bb C# G

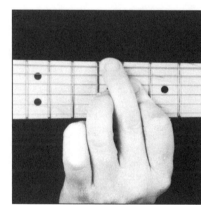

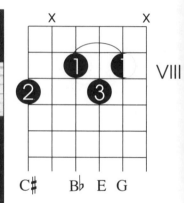

VIII

C#   Bb E G

C# major7

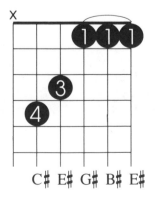

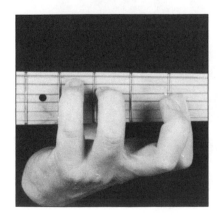

C# E# G# B# E#

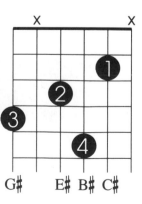

G#   E# B# C#

D♭7

D♭   F   A♭   C♭

D♭7 *first inversion*

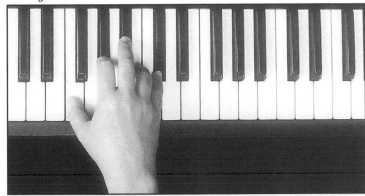

F   A♭   C♭   D♭

D♭°7

D♭   F♭   A♭♭   C♭♭

D♭°7 *first inversion*

F♭   A♭♭   C♭♭   D♭

D♭ major7

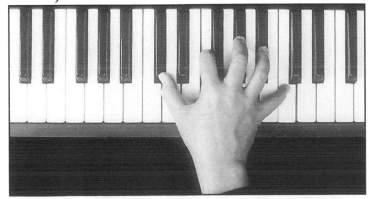

D♭   F   A♭   C

D♭ major7 *first inversion*

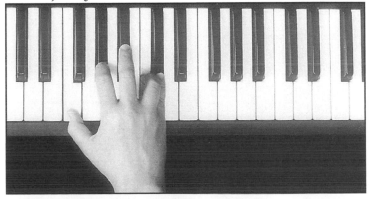

F   A♭   C D♭

C# minor

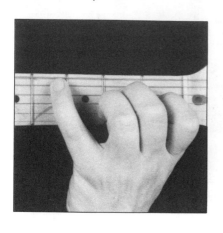

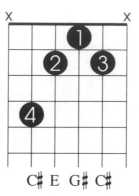

C# E G# C#

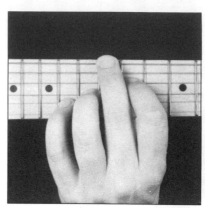

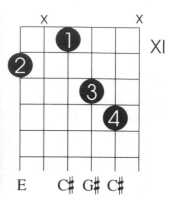

XI

E   C# G# C#

C# minor6

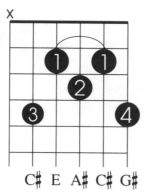

C# E A# C# G#

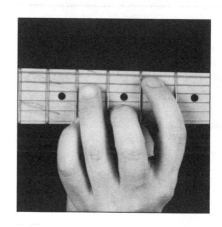

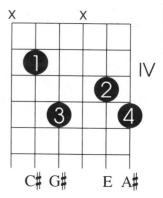

IV

C# G#   E A#

C# minor7

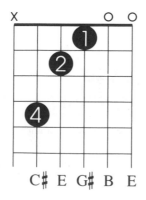

C# E G# B E

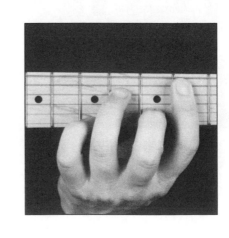

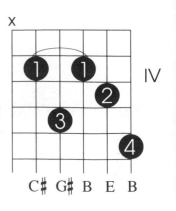

IV

C# G# B E B

Db minor

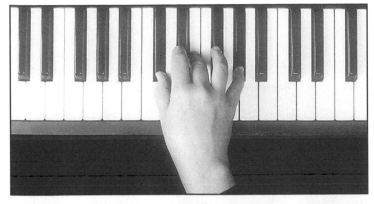

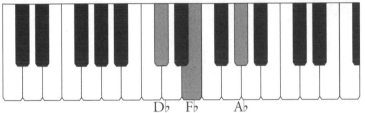

Db Fb Ab

Db minor *first inversion*

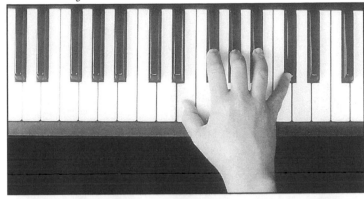

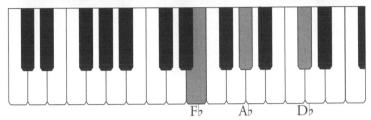

Fb Ab Db

Db minor6

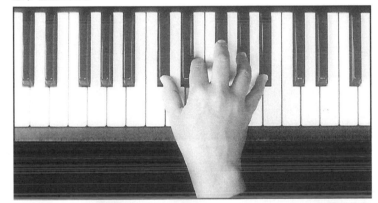

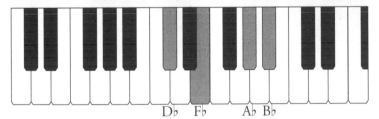

Db Fb Ab Bb

Db minor6 *first inversion*

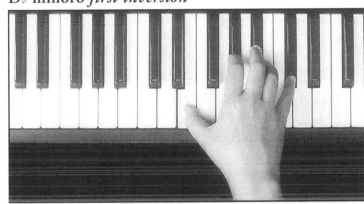

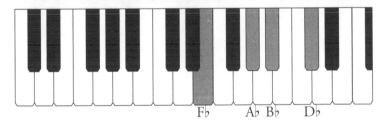

Fb Ab Bb Db

Db minor7

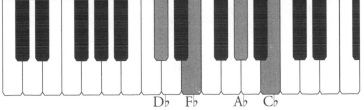

Db Fb Ab Cb

Db minor7 *first inversion*

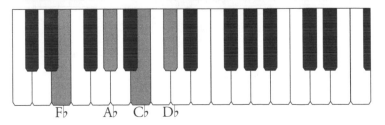

Fb Ab Cb Db

C# minor7b5

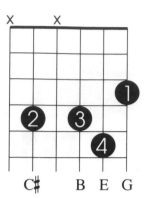

C#   B E G

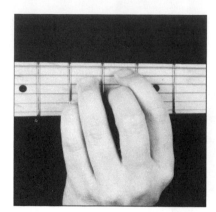

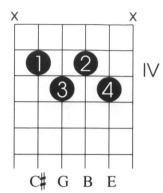

IV

C# G B E

C# minor (major7)

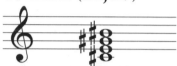

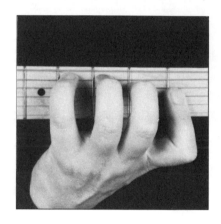

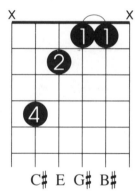

C# E G# B#

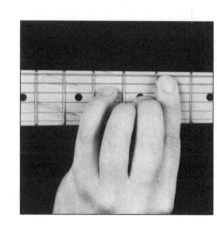

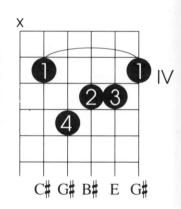

IV

C# G# B# E G#

D♭ minor7♭5

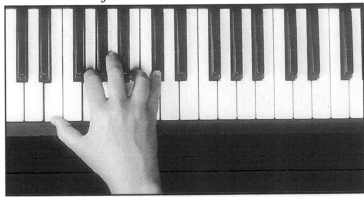

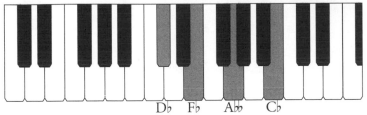

D♭ F♭ A♭♭ C♭

D♭ minor7♭5 *first inversion*

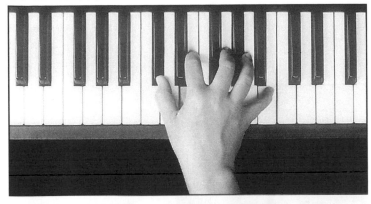

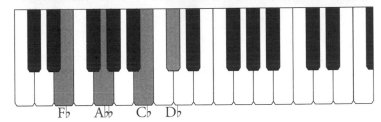

F♭ A♭♭ C♭ D♭

D♭ minor (major7)

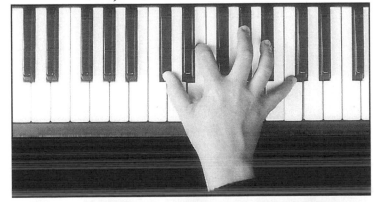

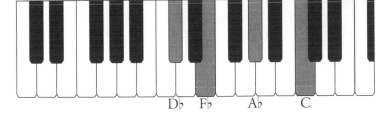

D♭ F♭ A♭ C

D♭ minor (major7) *first inversion*

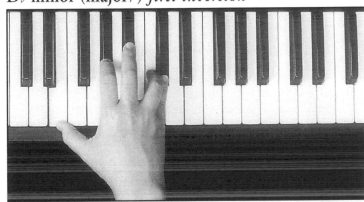

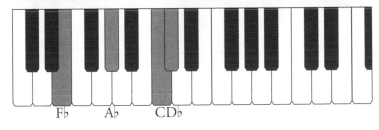

F♭ A♭ C D♭

C♯6/9

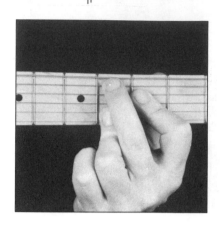
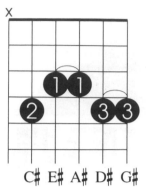

C♯ E♯ A♯ D♯ G♯

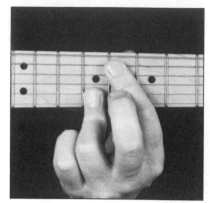
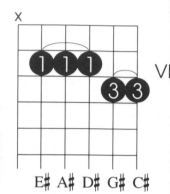

E♯ A♯ D♯ G♯ C♯
VI

C♯9

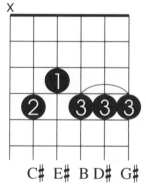

C♯ E♯ B D♯ G♯

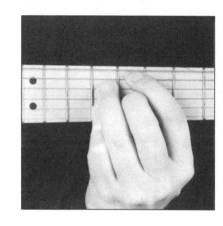
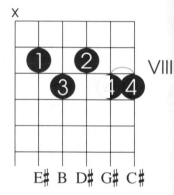

E♯ B D♯ G♯ C♯
VIII

C♯9sus4

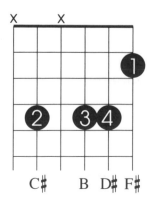

C♯ B D♯ F♯

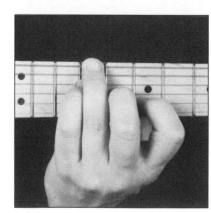
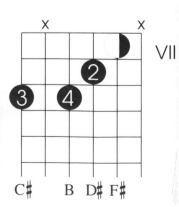

C♯ B D♯ F♯
VII

D♭6/9

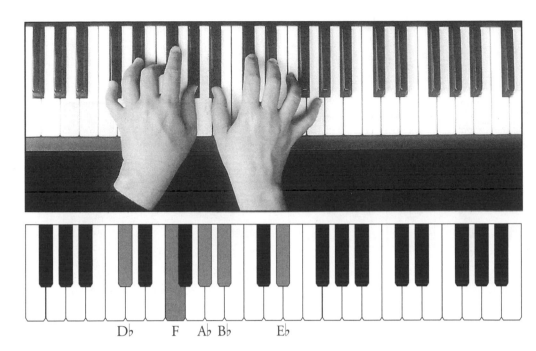

D♭   F A♭ B♭   E♭

D♭9

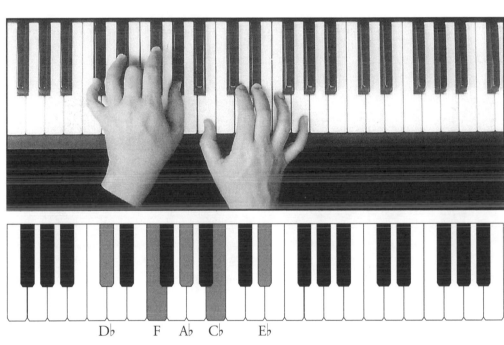

D♭   F A♭ C♭   E♭

D♭9sus4

C#9b5

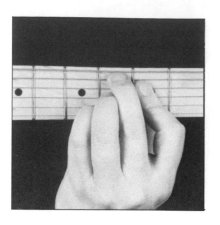

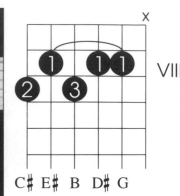

VIII

C# E# B D# G

C# E# B D# G

C#9#5

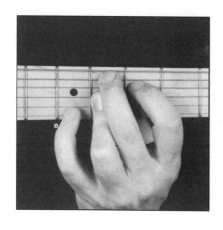

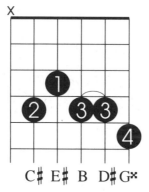

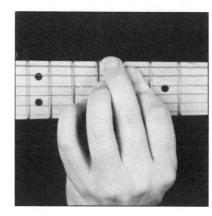

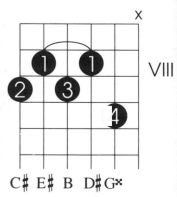

VIII

C# E# B D# G𝄪

C# E# B D# G𝄪

C#13

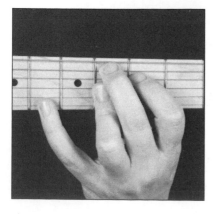

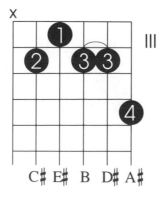

III

C# E# B D# A#

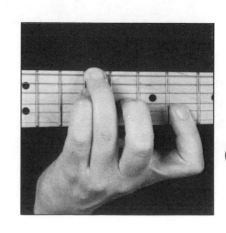

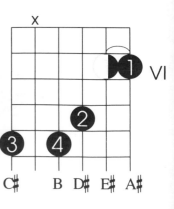

VI

C# B D# E# A#

Db9b5

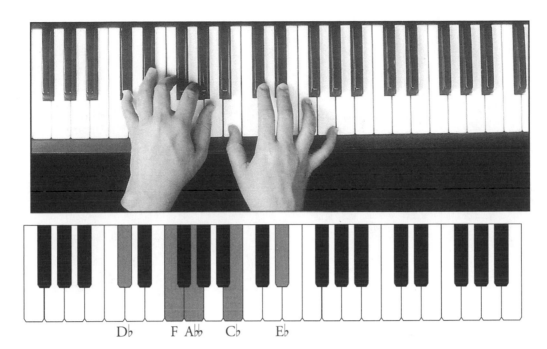

Db Ab F Abb Cb Eb

Db9#5

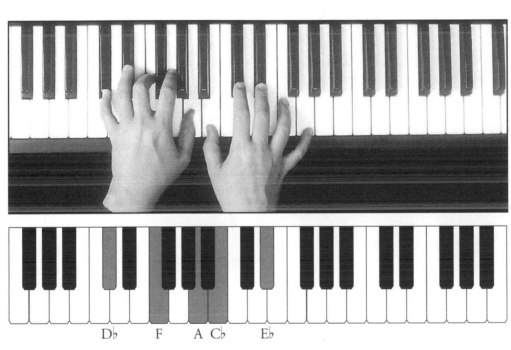

Db F A Cb Eb

Db13

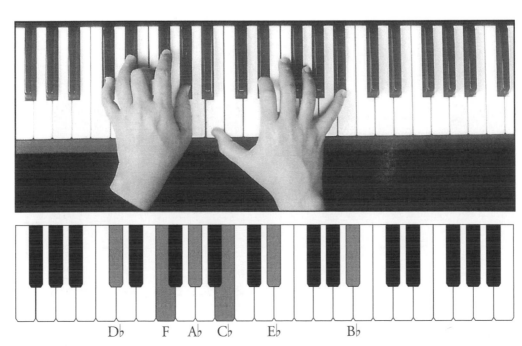

Db F Ab Cb Eb Bb

C# major9

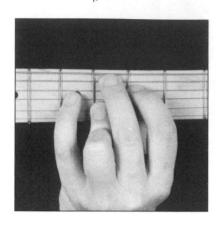

C# E# B# D# G#

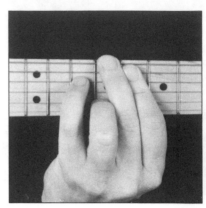

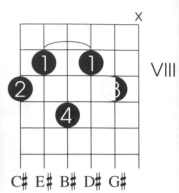

VIII

C# E# B# D# G#

C# major13

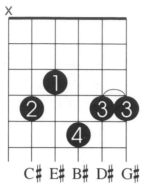

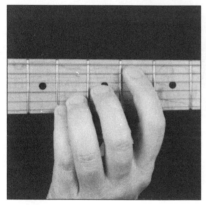

IV

C# B# E# A#

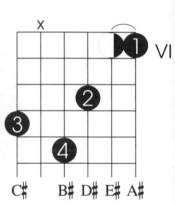

VI

C# B# D# E# A#

C# minor9

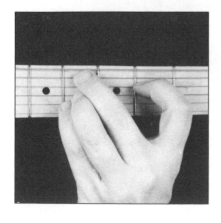

C# E B D#

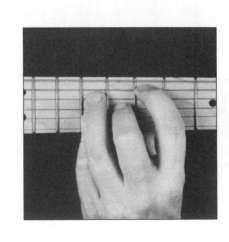

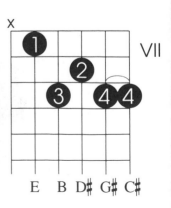

VII

E B D# G# C#

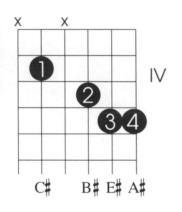

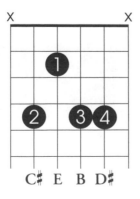

Db major9

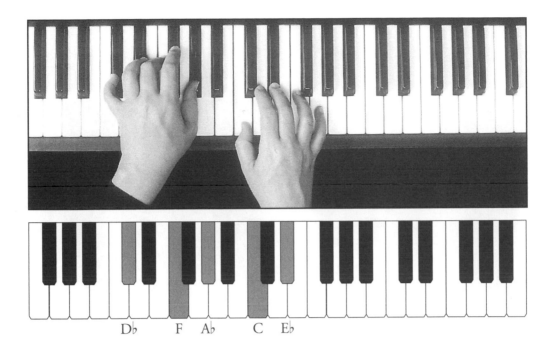

Db   F   Ab   C   Eb

Db major13

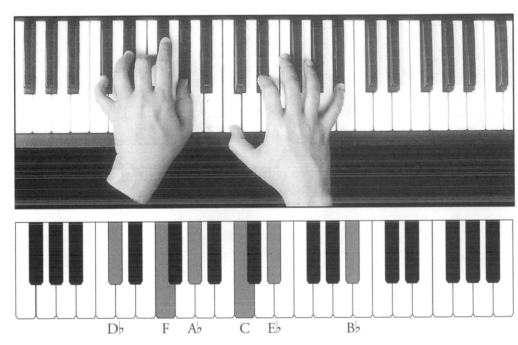

Db   F   Ab   C   Eb   Bb

Db minor9

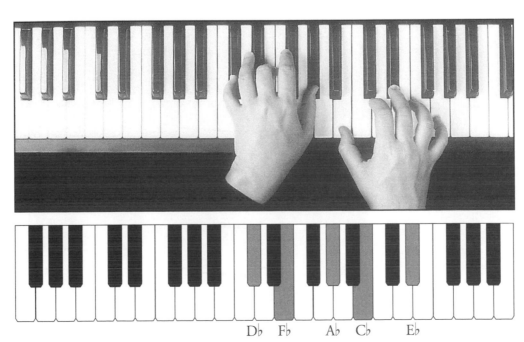

Db   Fb   Ab   Cb   Eb

C# minor11

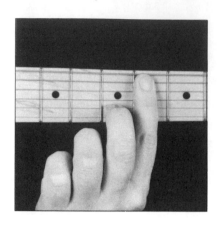

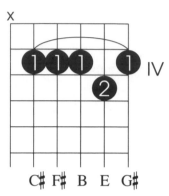

IV

C# F# B E G#

C# E B D# F#

C# minor13

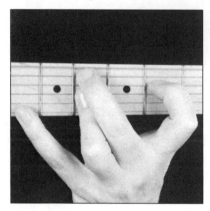

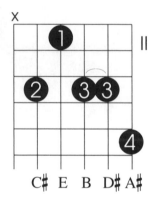

II

C# E B D# A#

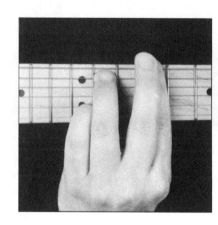

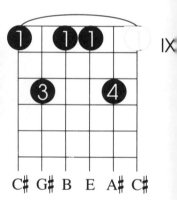

IX

C# G# B E A# C#

D♭ minor11

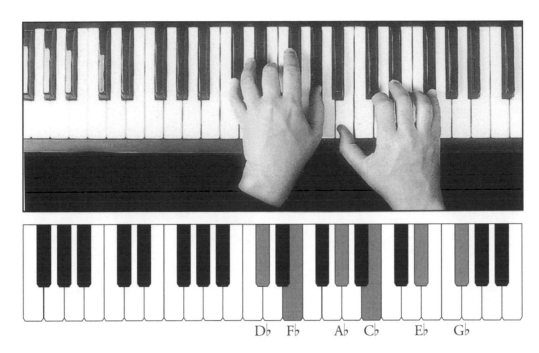

D♭   F♭   A♭   C♭   E♭   G♭

D♭ minor13

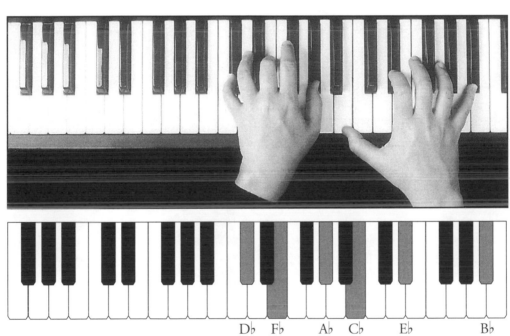

D♭   F♭   A♭   C♭   E♭   B♭

D Chords

D major

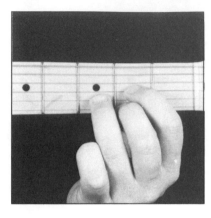 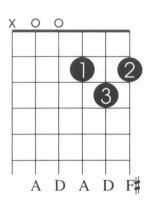

 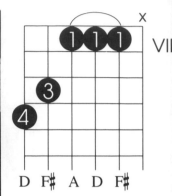

Dsus4

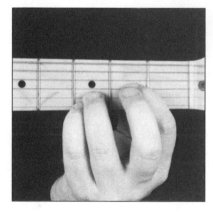 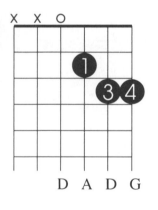

 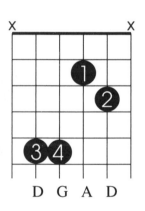

D6

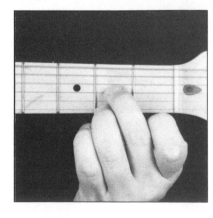 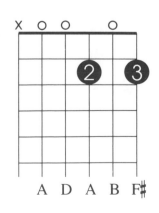

 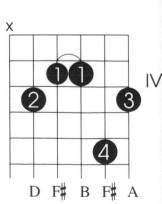

D major

D F♯ A

D major *first inversion*

F♯ A D

Dsus4

D G A

Dsus4 *first inversion*

G A D

D6

D F♯ A B

D6 *first inversion*

F♯ A B D

D7

X O O

A D A C F#

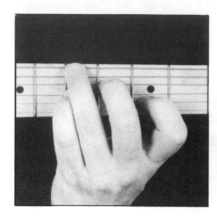

X

III

A D F# C D

D°7

X X O O

D A♭ C♭ F

X X

A♭ F C♭ D

D major7

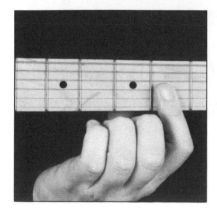

X O O

A D A C# F#

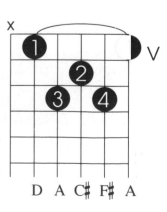

X

V

D A C# F# A

D7

D7 *first inversion*

D F♯ A C

F♯ A C D

D°7

D°7 *first inversion*

D F A♭ C♭

F A♭ C♭ D

D major7

D major7 *first inversion*

D F♯ A C♯

F♯ A C♯ D

D minor

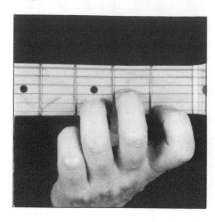

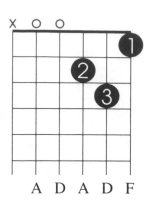

A D A D F

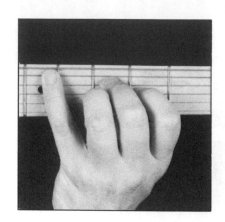

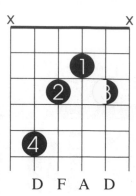

D F A D

D minor6

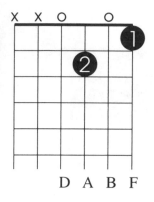

D A B F

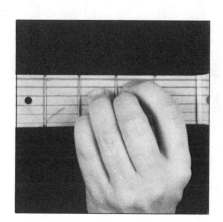

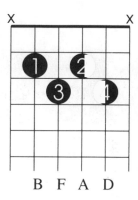

B F A D

D minor7

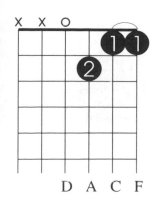

D A C F

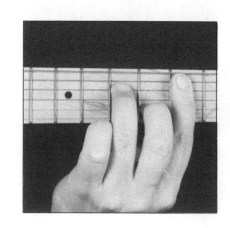

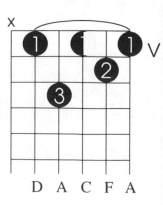

D A C F A

D minor

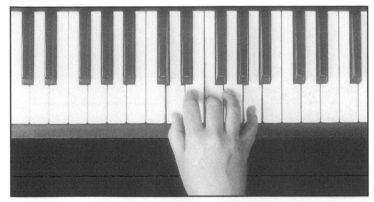

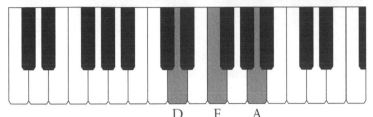

D F A

D minor *first inversion*

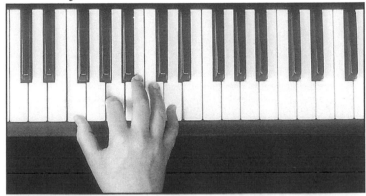

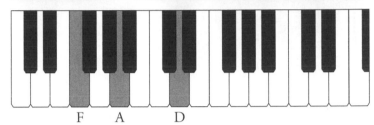

F A D

D minor6

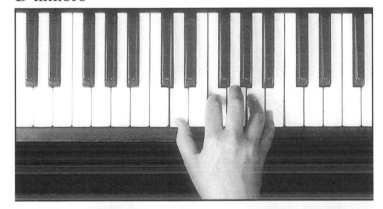

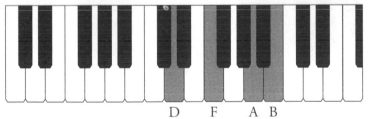

D F A B

D minor6 *first inversion*

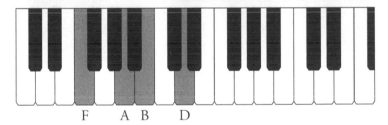

F A B D

D minor7

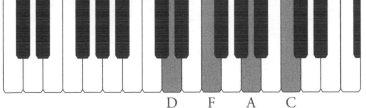

D F A C

D minor7 *first inversion*

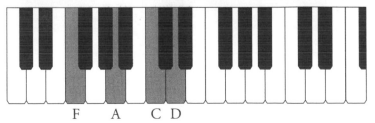

F A C D

D minor7♭5

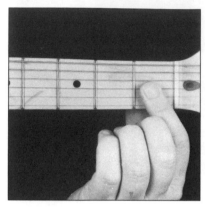

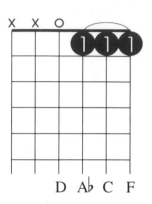

D A♭ C F

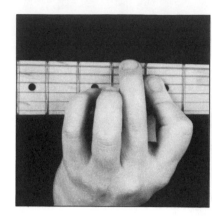

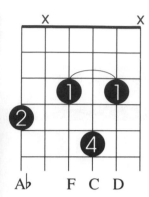

A♭ F C D

D minor (major7)

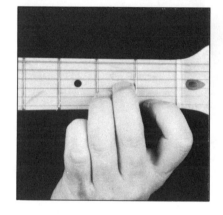

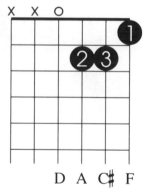

D A C♯ F

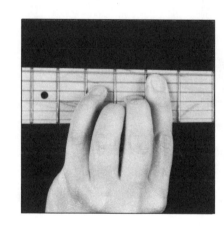

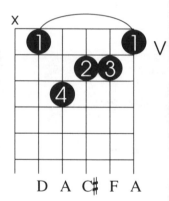

D A C♯ F A — V

D minor7♭5

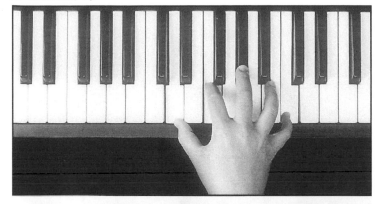

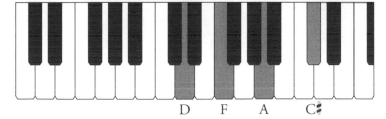

D   F   A♭   C

D minor7♭5 *first inversion*

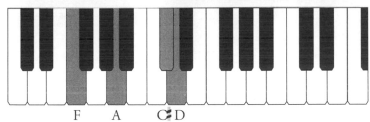

F   A♭   C   D

D minor (major7)

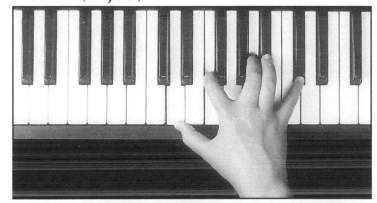

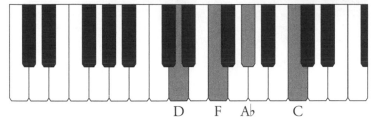

D   F   A   C♯

D minor (major7) *first inversion*

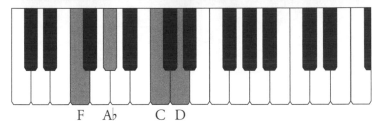

F   A   C♯ D

D6/9

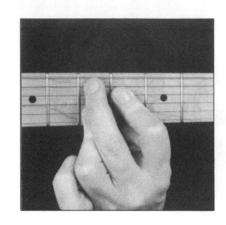

D F# A B E

D F# B E A

IV

D9

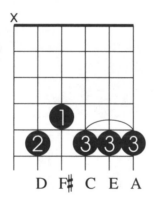

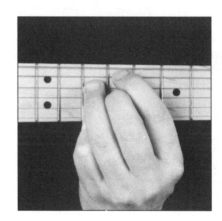

D F# C E A

F# C E A D

IX

D9sus4

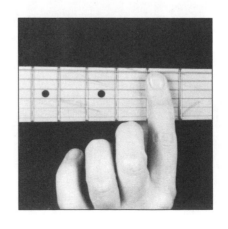

D C E G

D G C E A

V

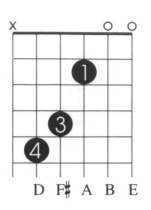
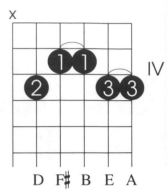
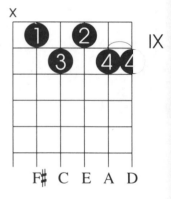
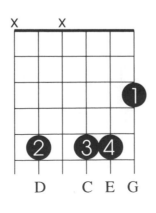
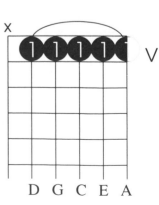
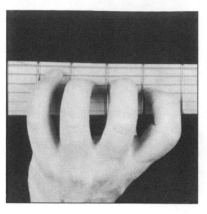

D6/9

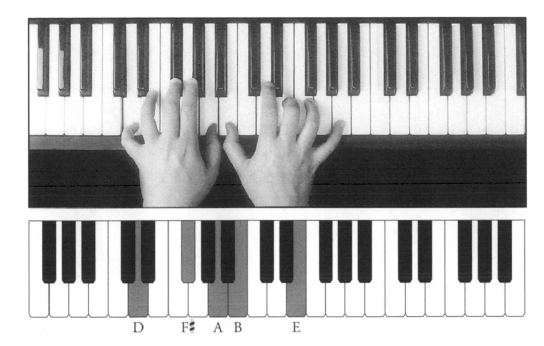

D   F♯ A B   E

D9

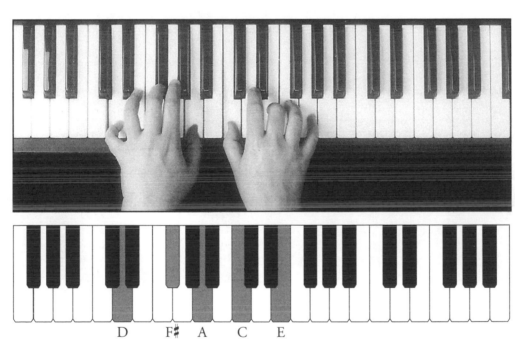

D   F♯   A   C   E

D9sus4

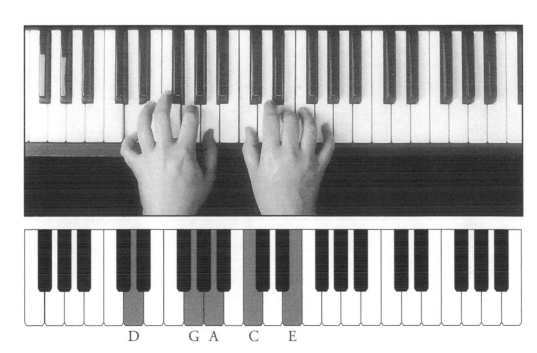

D   G A   C   E

D9♭5

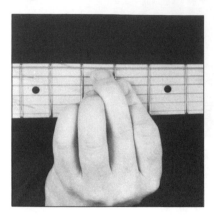

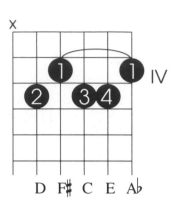

D F♯ C E A♭   IV

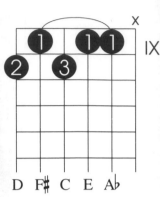

D F♯ C E A♭   IX

D9♯5

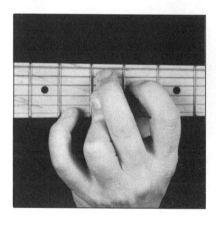

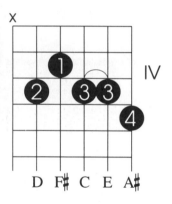

D F♯ C E A♯   IV

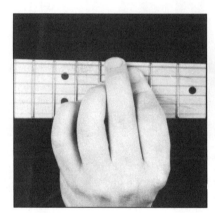

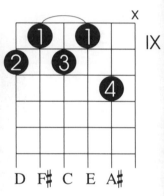

D F♯ C E A♯   IX

D13

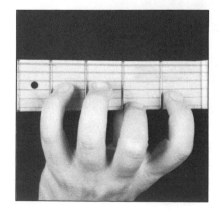

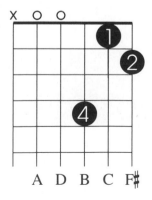

A D B C F♯

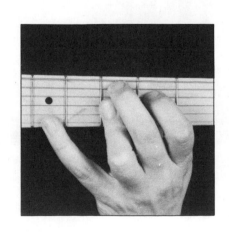

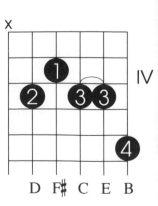

D F♯ C E B   IV

D9♭5

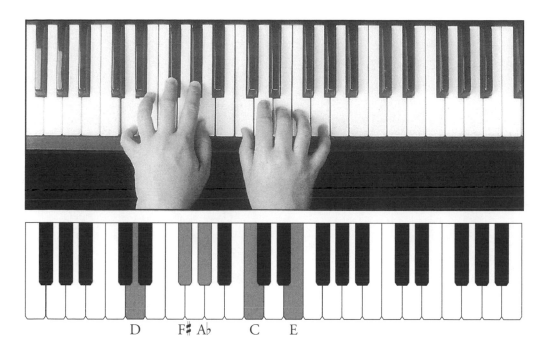

D   F# A♭   C   E

D9♯5

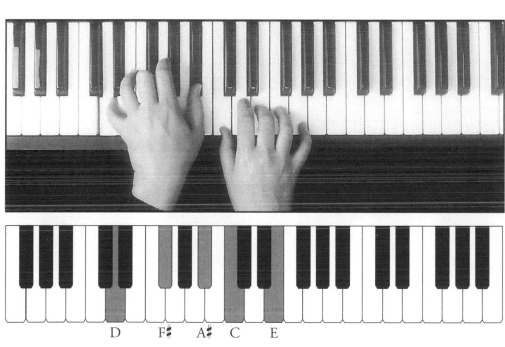

D   F#   A#   C   E

D13

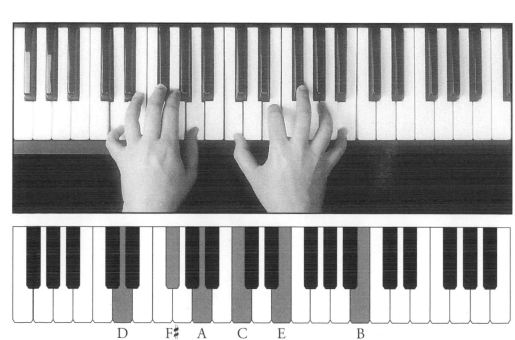

D   F#   A   C   E   B

D major9

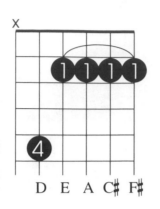

D E A C# F#

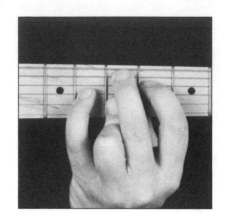
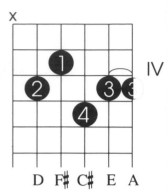

IV

D F# C# E A

D major13

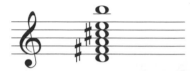

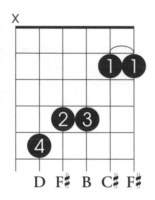

D F# B C# F#

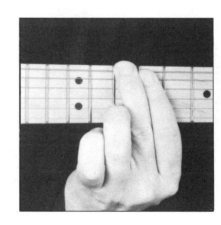
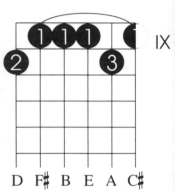

IX

D F# B E A C#

D minor9

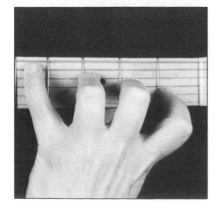
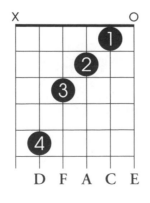

D F A C E

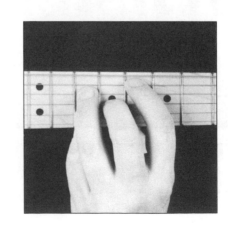
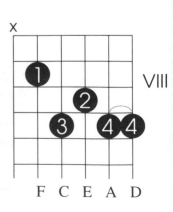

VIII

F C E A D

D major9

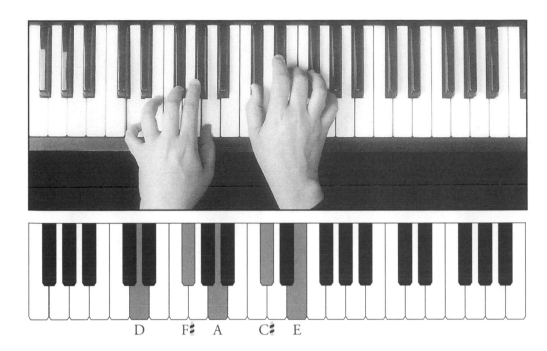

D   F♯   A   C♯ E

D major13

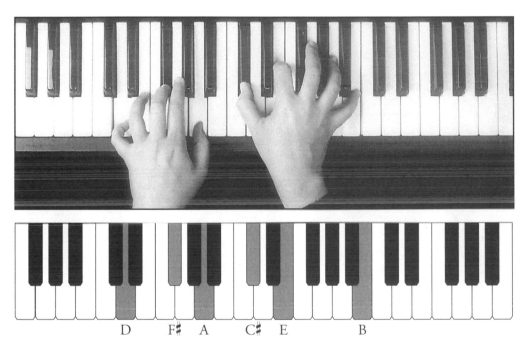

D   F♯   A   C♯ E   B

D minor9

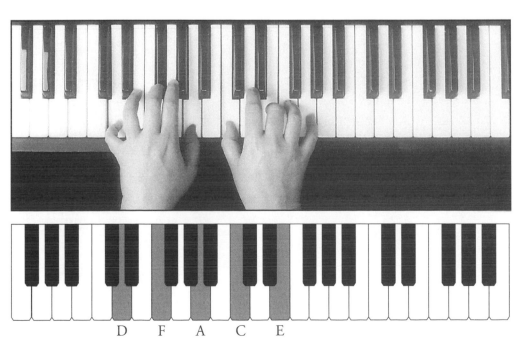

D   F   A   C   E

D minor11

 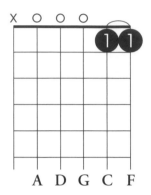

A D G C F

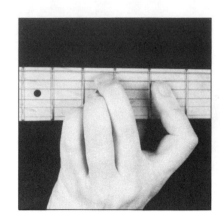 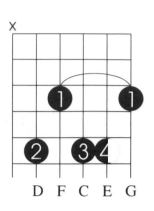

D F C E G

D minor13

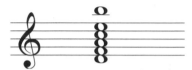

 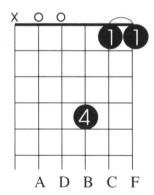

A D B C F

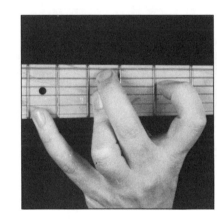 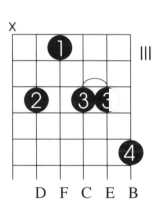

D F C E B

D minor11

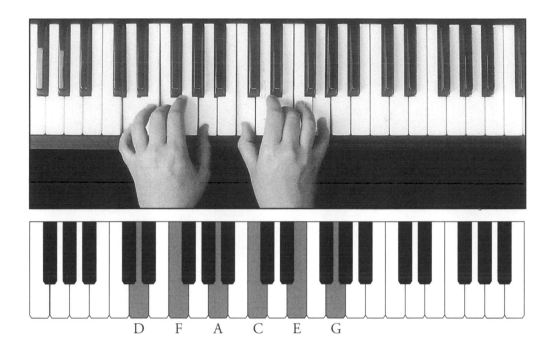

D F A C E G

D minor13

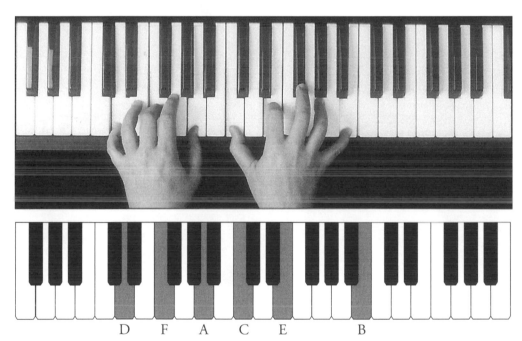

D F A C E B

E♭ Chords

E♭ major

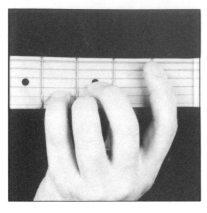

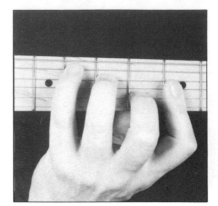

Bb Eb Bb Eb G

Eb G Bb Eb G

III

E♭sus4

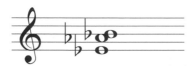

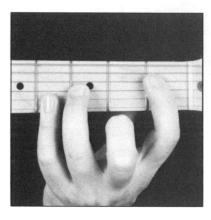

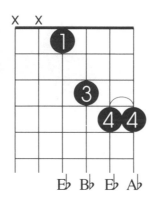

Eb Bb Eb Ab

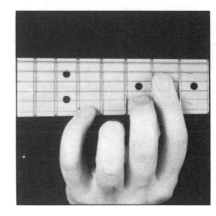

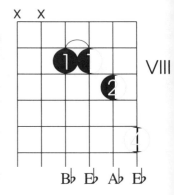

Bb Eb Ab Eb

VIII

E♭6

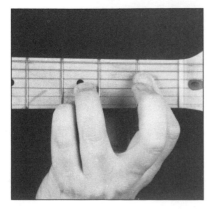

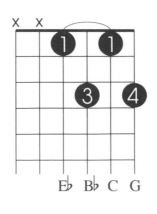

Eb Bb C G

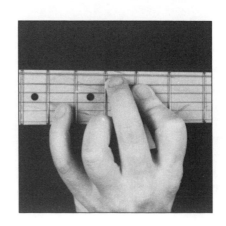

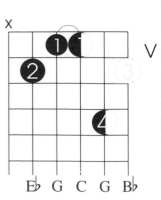

Eb G C G Bb

V

62

E♭ major

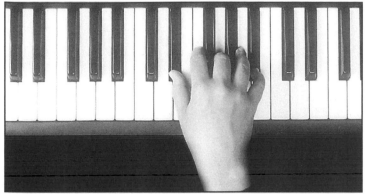

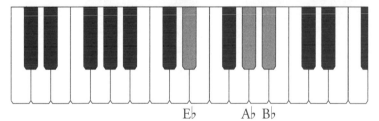

E♭ G B♭

E♭ major *first inversion*

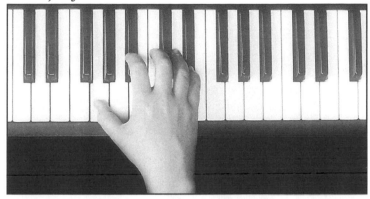

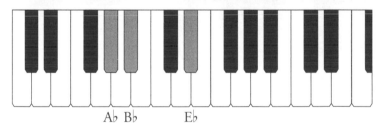

G B♭ E♭

E♭sus4

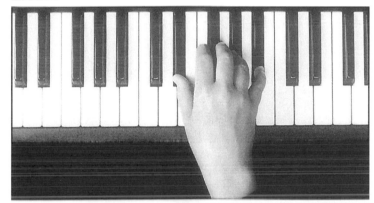

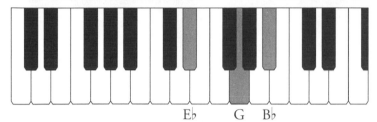

E♭ A♭ B♭

E♭sus4 *first inversion*

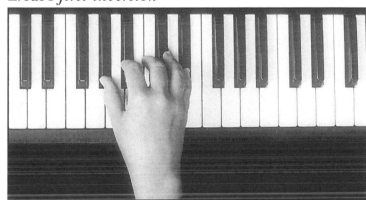

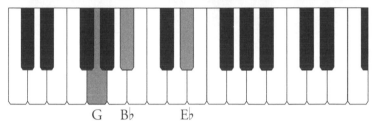

A♭ B♭ E♭

E♭6

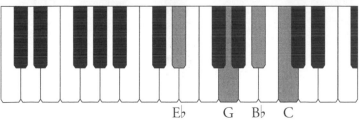

E♭ G B♭ C

E♭6 *first inversion*

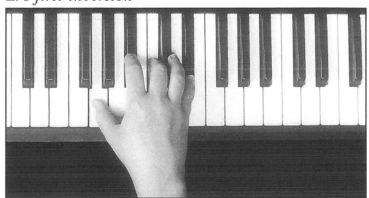

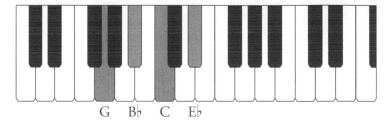

G B♭ C E♭

E♭7

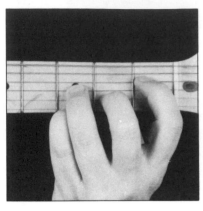

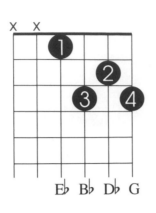

Eb Bb Db G

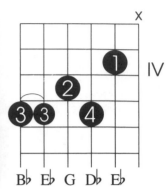

IV

Bb Eb G Db Eb

E♭°7

Eb Bb♭ Db♭ Gb

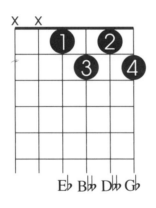

V

Eb Bb♭ Db♭ Gb

E♭ major7

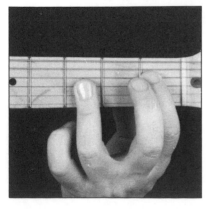

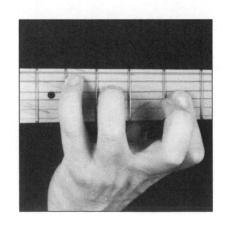

Eb Bb D G

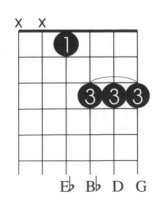

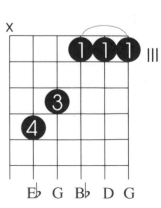

III

Eb G Bb D G

E♭7

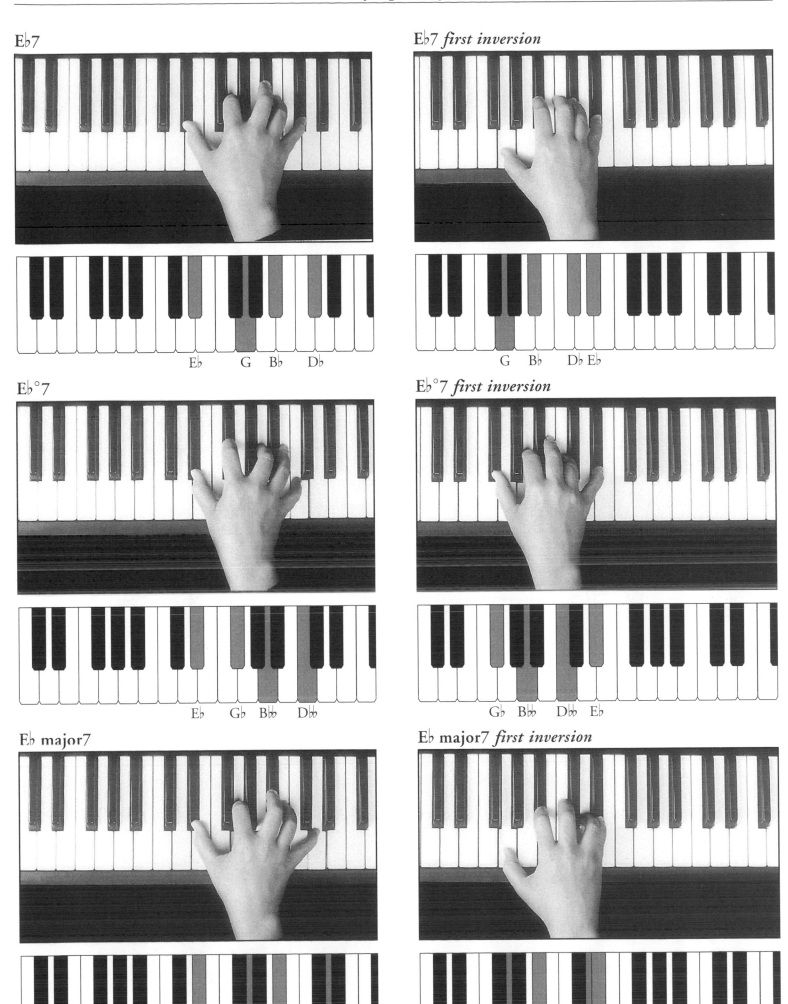

E♭ G B♭ D♭

E♭7 *first inversion*

G B♭ D♭ E♭

E♭°7

E♭ G♭ B♭♭ D♭♭

E♭°7 *first inversion*

G♭ B♭♭ D♭♭ E♭

E♭ major7

E♭ G B♭ D

E♭ major7 *first inversion*

G B♭ D E♭

Eb minor

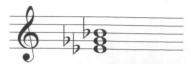

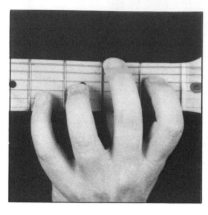
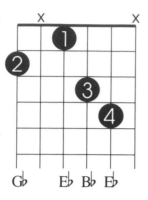

Gb Eb Bb Eb

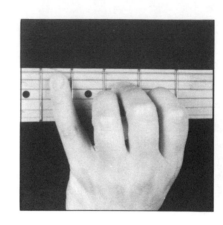
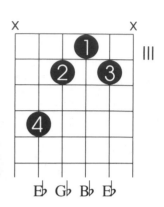

III

Eb Gb Bb Eb

Eb minor6

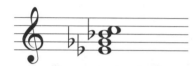

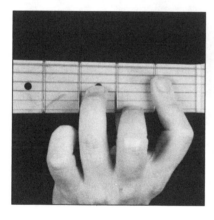
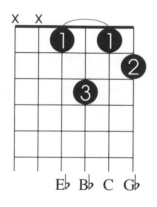

Eb Bb C Gb

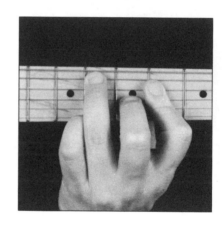
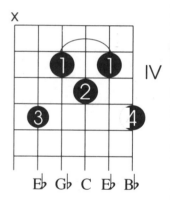

IV

Eb Gb C Eb Bb

Eb minor7

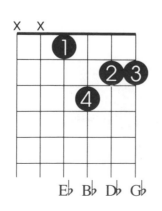

Eb Bb Db Gb

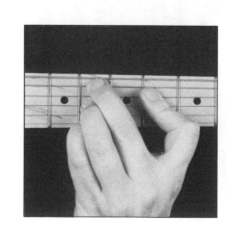
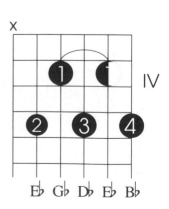

IV

Eb Gb Db Eb Bb

E♭ minor

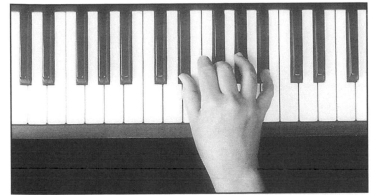

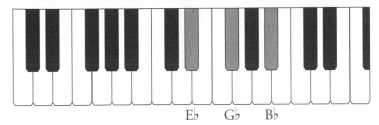

E♭ G♭ B♭

E♭ minor *first inversion*

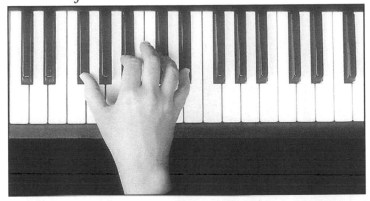

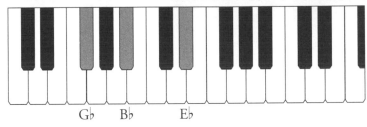

G♭ B♭ E♭

E♭ minor6

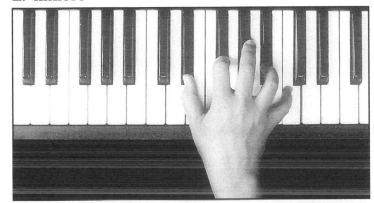

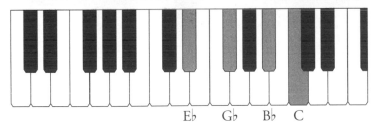

E♭ G♭ B♭ C

E♭ minor6 *first inversion*

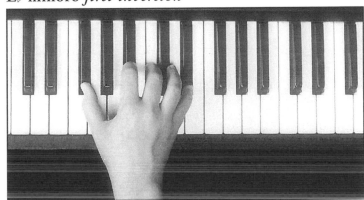

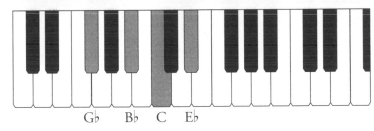

G♭ B♭ C E♭

E♭ minor7

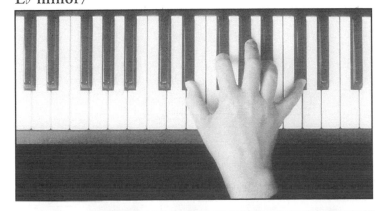

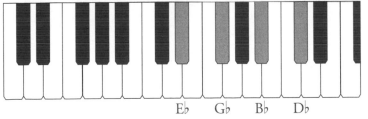

E♭ G♭ B♭ D♭

E♭ minor7 *first inversion*

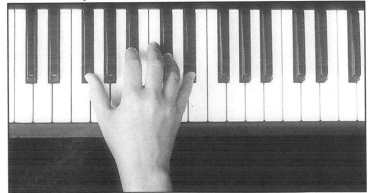

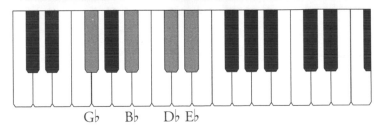

G♭ B♭ D♭ E♭

Eb minor7b5

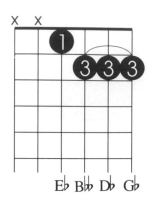

Eb Bb Db Gb

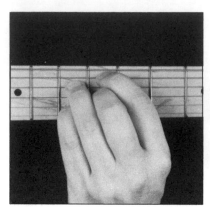
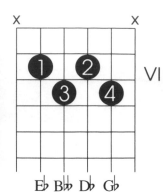

VI

Eb Bb Db Gb

Eb minor (major7)

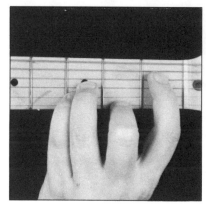
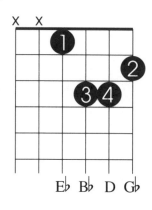

Eb Bb D Gb

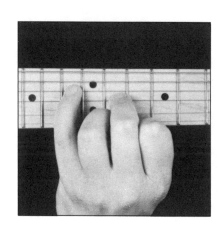
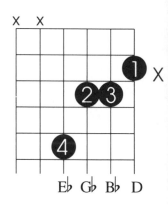

Eb Gb Bb D

E♭ minor7♭5

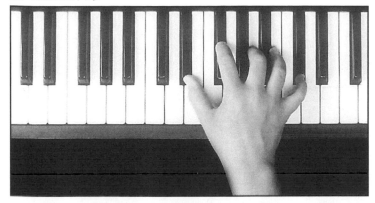

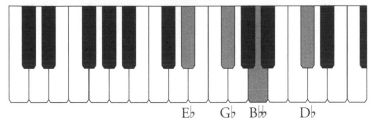

E♭ G♭ B♭♭ D♭

E♭ minor7♭5 *first inversion*

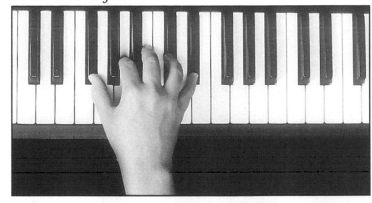

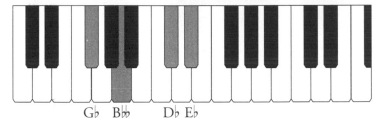

G♭ B♭♭ D♭ E♭

E♭ minor (major7)

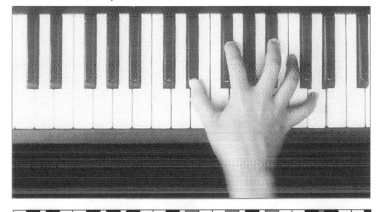

E♭ G♭ B♭ D

E♭ minor (major7) *first inversion*

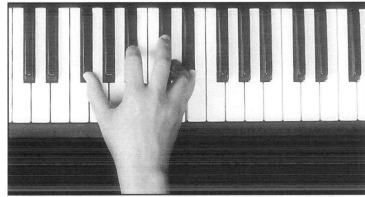

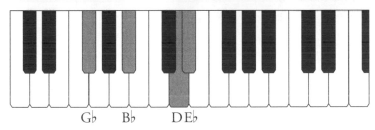

G♭ B♭ D E♭

E♭6/9

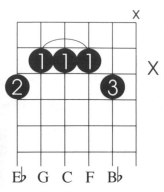

Eb Gb Db F

E♭9

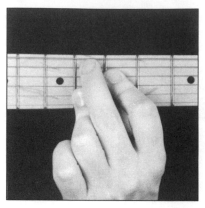

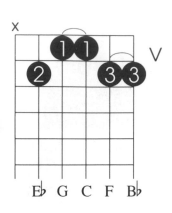

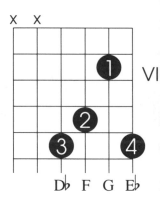

E♭9sus4

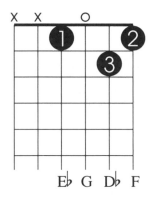

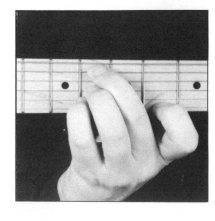

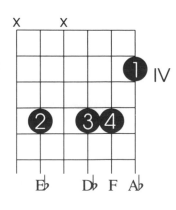

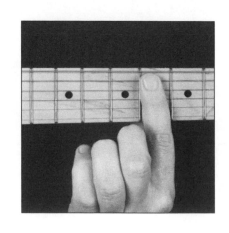

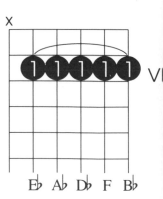

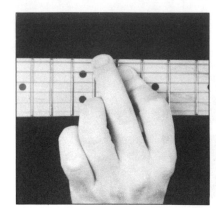

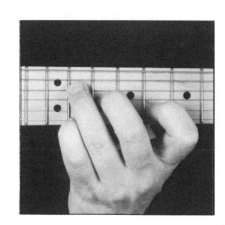

Eb6/9

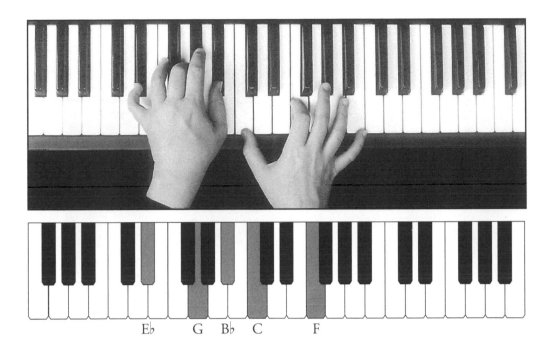

Eb   G   Bb   C   F

Eb9

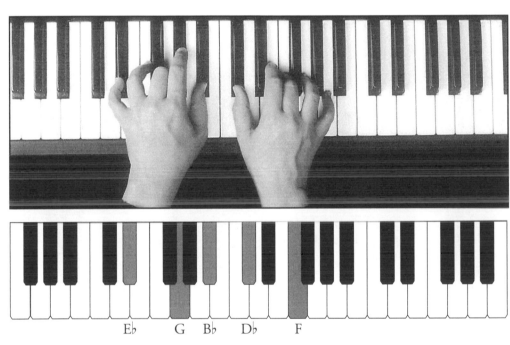

Eb   G   Bb   Db   F

Eb9sus4

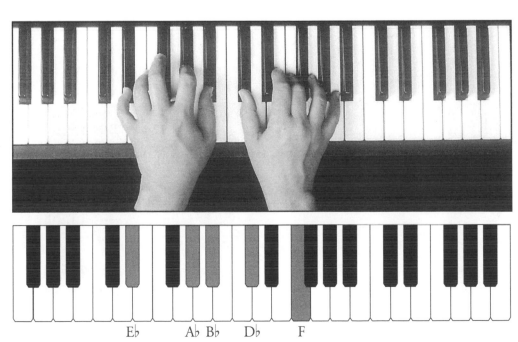

Eb   Ab   Bb   Db   F

E♭9♭5

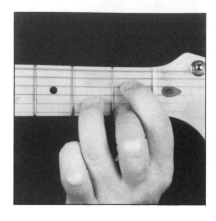

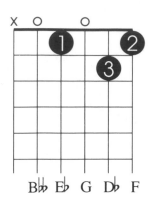

B♭♭ E♭ G D♭ F

E♭ G D♭ F B♭♭

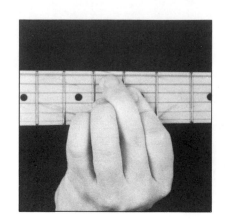

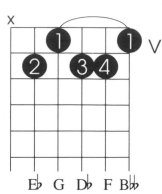

E♭9♯5

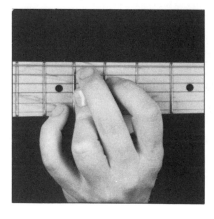

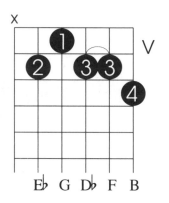

E♭ G D♭ F B

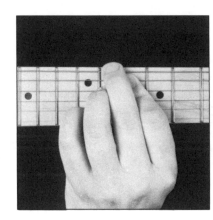

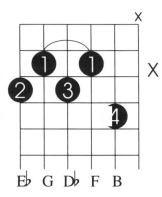

E♭ G D♭ F B

E♭13

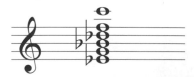

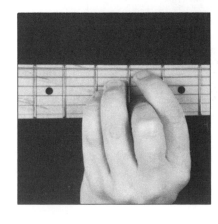

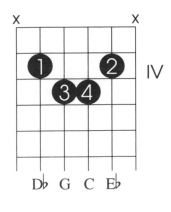

D♭ G C E♭

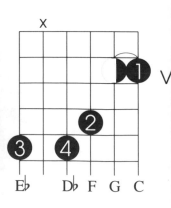

E♭ D♭ F G C

Eb9b5

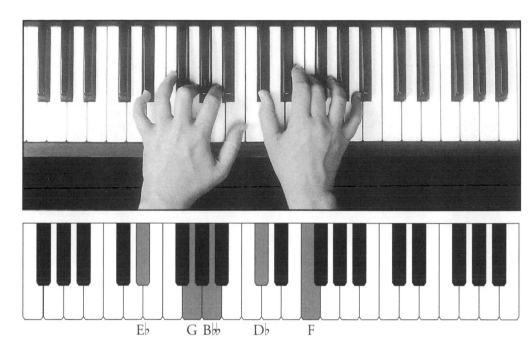

Eb G Bbb   Db   F

Eb9#5

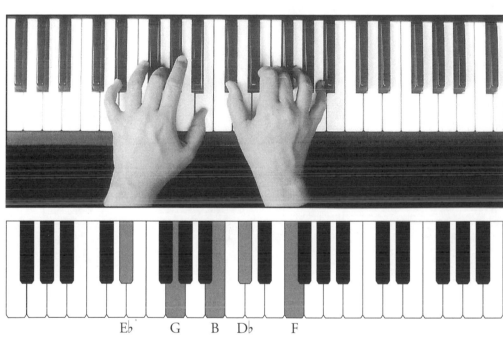

Eb   G   B   Db   F

Eb13

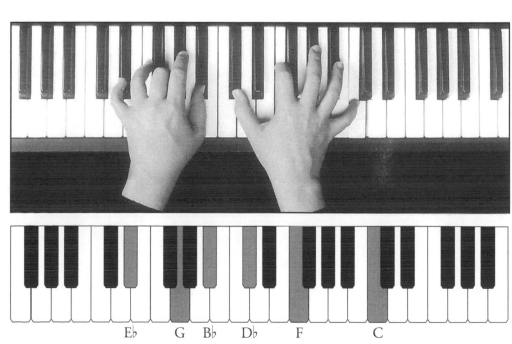

Eb   G   Bb   Db   F   C

E♭ major9

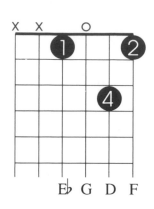

Eb G D F

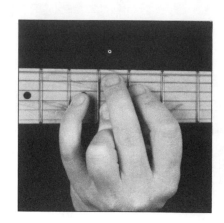
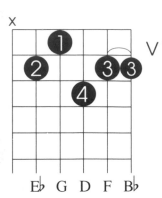

V

Eb G D F Bb

E♭ major13

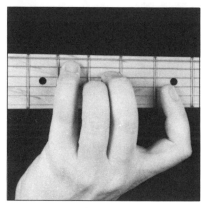
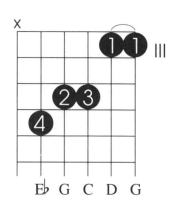

III

Eb G C D G

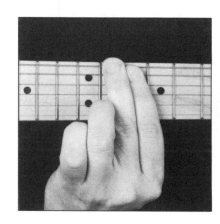
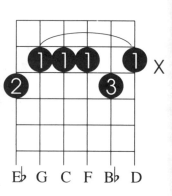

X

Eb G C F Bb D

E♭ minor9

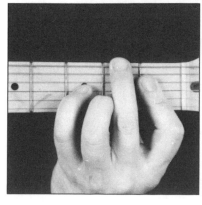
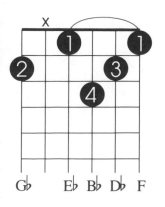

Gb Eb Bb Db F

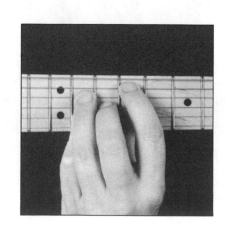
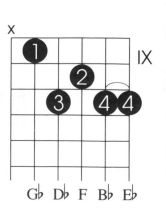

IX

Gb Db F Bb Eb

Eb major9

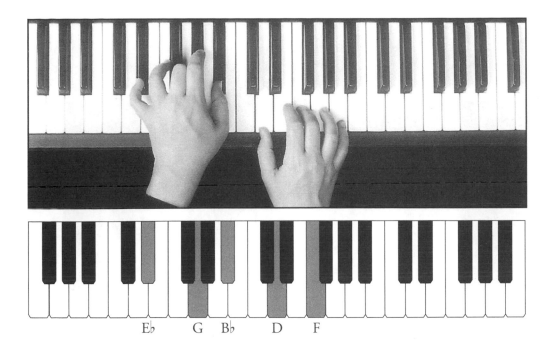

Eb   G   Bb   D   F

Eb major13

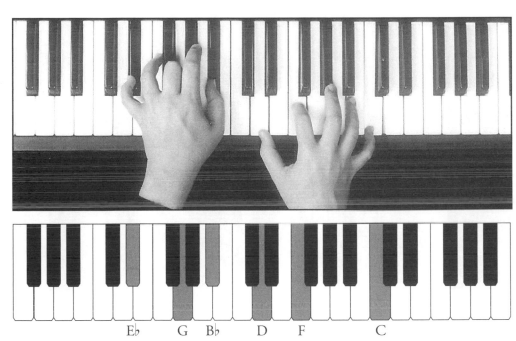

Eb   G   Bb   D   F   C

Eb minor9

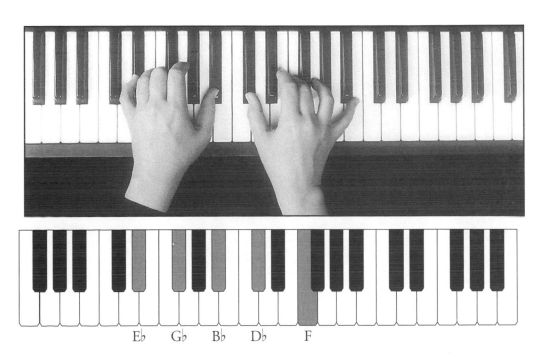

Eb   Gb   Bb   Db   F

E♭ minor11

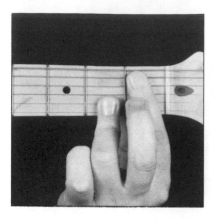
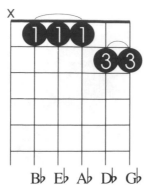

B♭ E♭ A♭ D♭ G♭

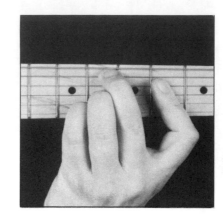
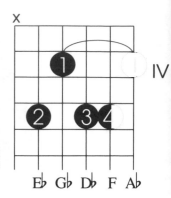

IV

E♭ G♭ D♭ F A♭

E♭ minor13

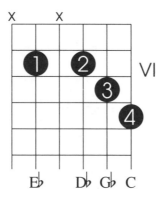

VI

E♭ D♭ G♭ C

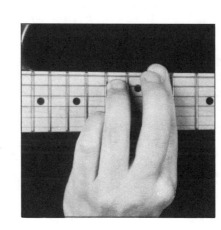
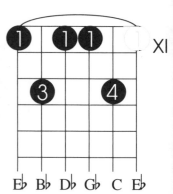

XI

E♭ B♭ D♭ G♭ C E♭

Eb minor11

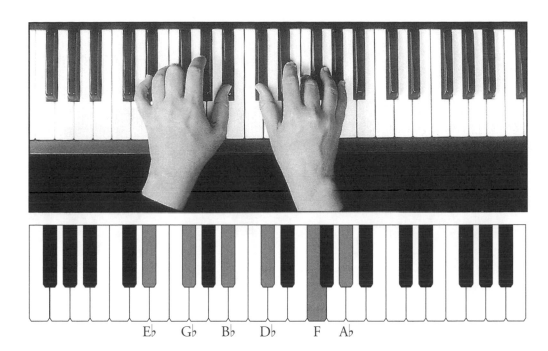

Eb   Gb   Bb   Db   F   Ab

Eb minor13

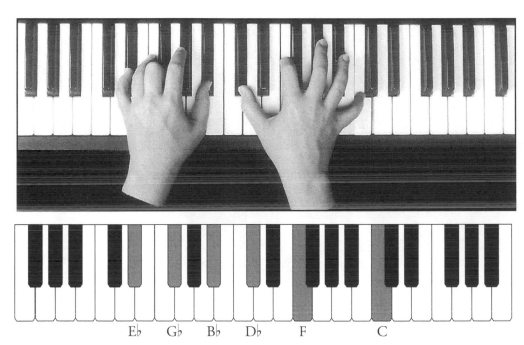

Eb   Gb   Bb   Db   F   C

E Chords

E major

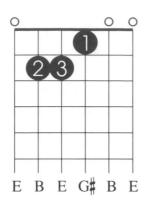

E B E G# B E

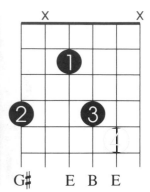

G#　E B E

Esus4

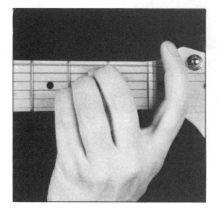
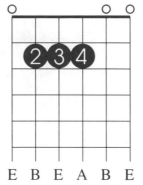

E B E A B E

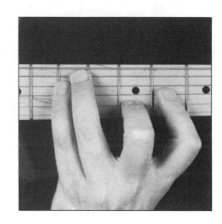

IV

E A B E

E6

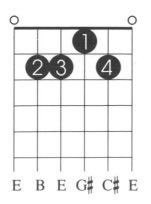

E B E G# C# E

V

B　G# C# E

E major

E   G♯   B

E major *first inversion*

G♯   B   E

Esus4

E   A B

Esus4 *first inversion*

A B   E

E6

E   G♯   B   C♯

E6 *first inversion*

G♯   B   C♯   E

E7

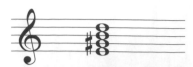

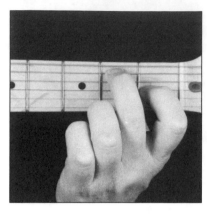

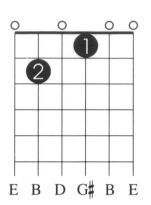

E B D G# B E

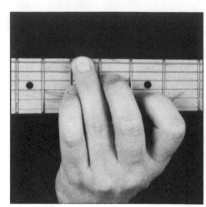

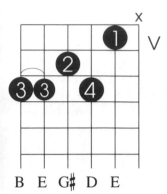

V

B E G# D E

E°7

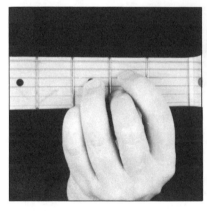

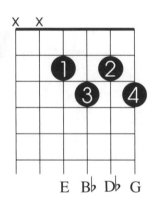

E B♭ D♭ G

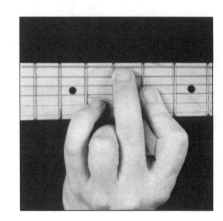

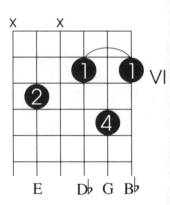

VI

E D♭ G B♭

E major7

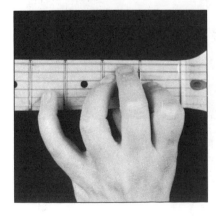

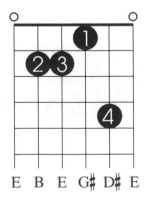

E B E G# D# E

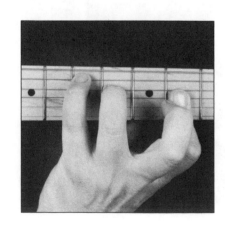

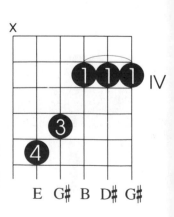

IV

E G# B D# G#

E7

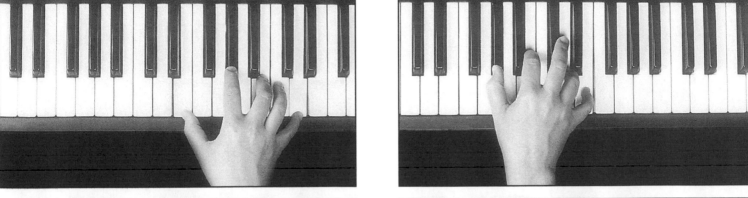

E   G♯   B   D

E7 *first inversion*

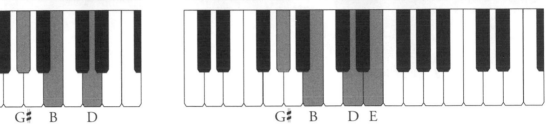

G♯   B   D   E

E°7

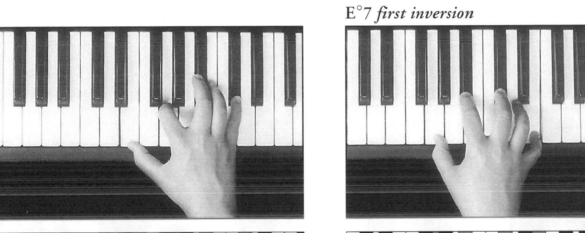

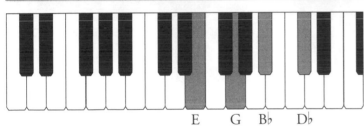

E   G   B♭   D♭

E°7 *first inversion*

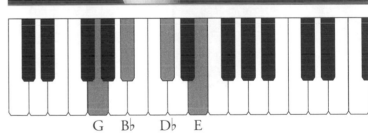

G   B♭   D♭   E

E major7

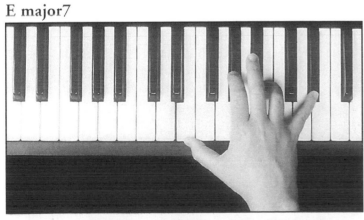

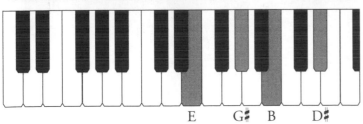

E   G♯   B   D♯

E major7 *first inversion*

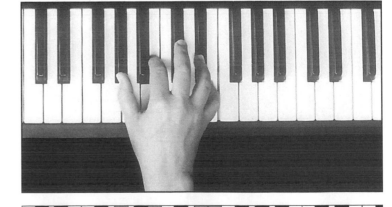

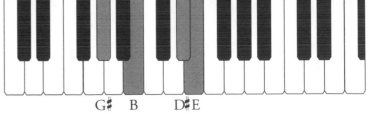

G♯   B   D♯ E

E minor

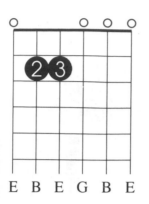

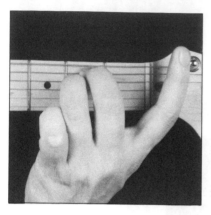

E B E G B E

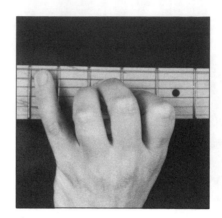

IV

E G B E

E minor6

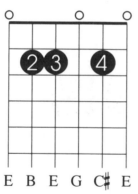

E B E G C♯ E

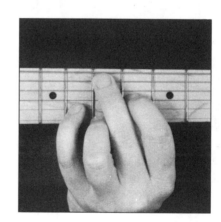

VI

E C♯ G B

E minor7

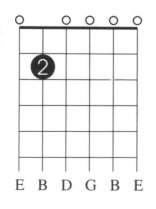

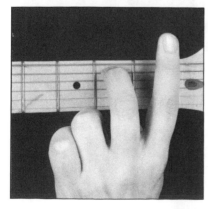

E B D G B E

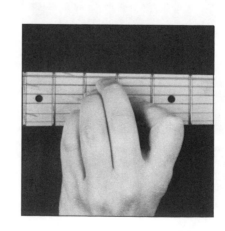

IV

D G B E

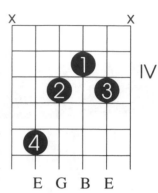

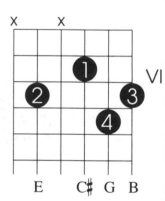

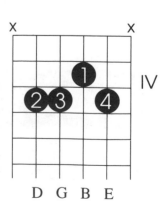

E minor

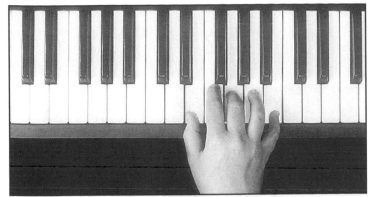
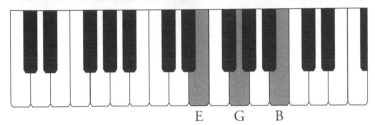

E　G　B

E minor *first inversion*

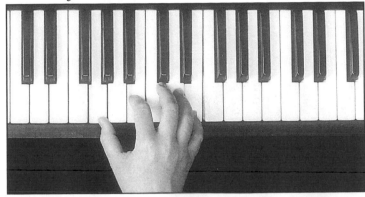
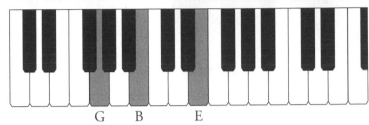

G　B　E

E minor6

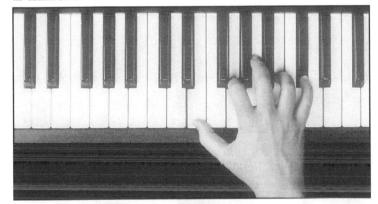
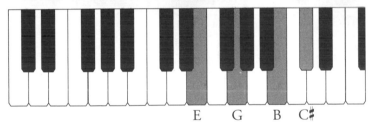

E　G　B　C♯

E minor6 *first inversion*

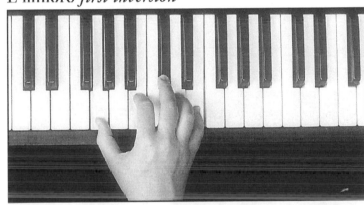
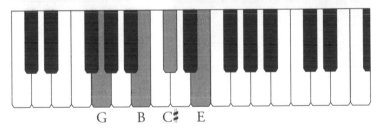

G　B　C♯　E

E minor7

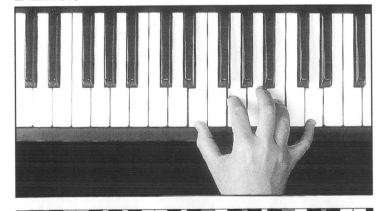

E　G　B　D

E minor7 *first inversion*

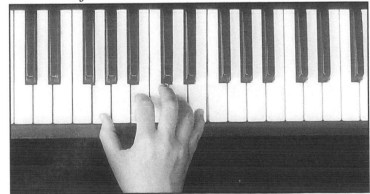
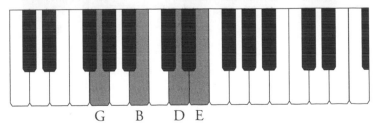

G　B　D　E

E minor7♭5

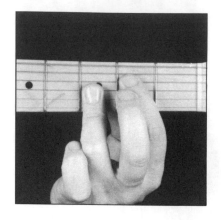 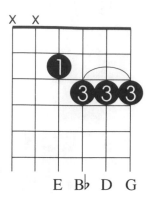

x x

E B♭ D G

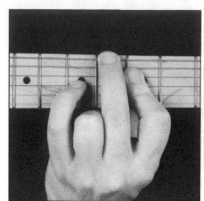 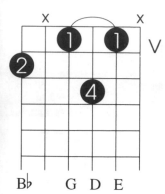

x x

V

B♭ G D E

E minor (major7)

 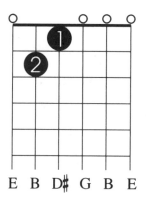

o o o o

E B D♯ G B E

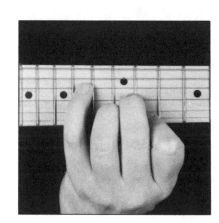 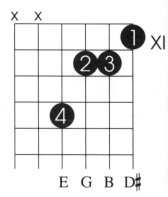

x x

XI

E G B D♯

E minor7♭5

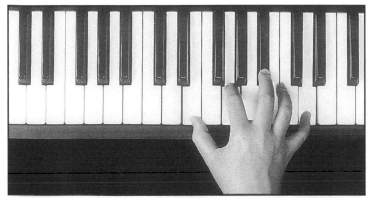

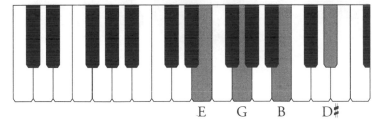

E   G   B♭   D

E minor7♭5 *first inversion*

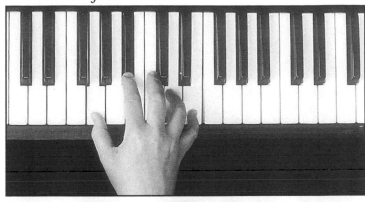

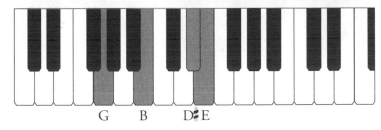

G   B♭   D   E

E minor (major7)

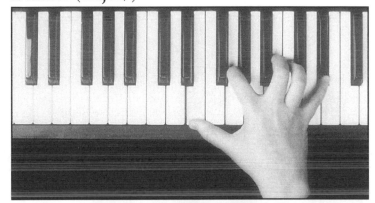

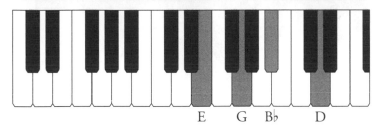

E   G   B   D♯

E minor (major7) *first inversion*

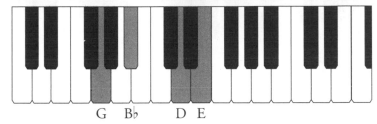

G   B   D♯ E

E6/9

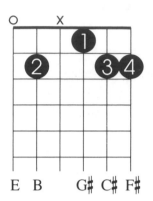

O   x

2   1   3 4

E B   G# C# F#

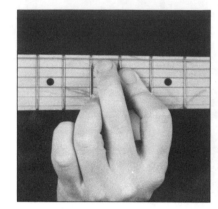

x   x

1 1
2   3   VI

E G# C# F#

E9

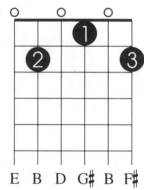

O   O   O

2   1   3

E B D G# B F#

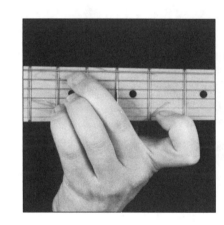
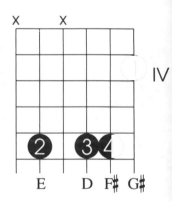

x   x

IV

2   3 4

E   D F# G#

E9sus4

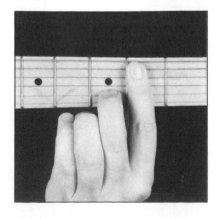
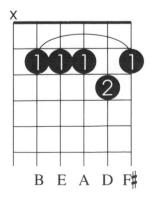

x

1 1 1   1
2

B E A D F#

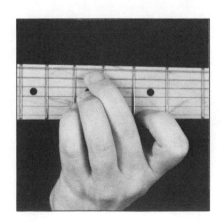
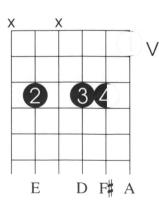

x   x

V

2   3 4

E   D F# A

E6/9

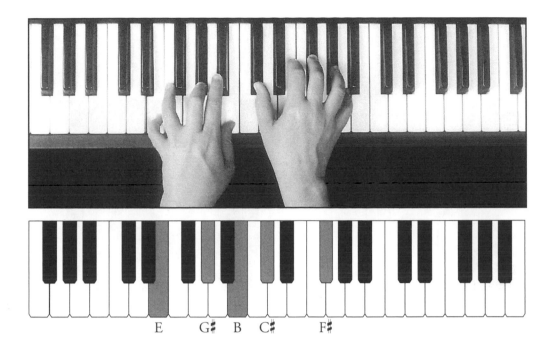

E   G♯   B   C♯   F♯

E9

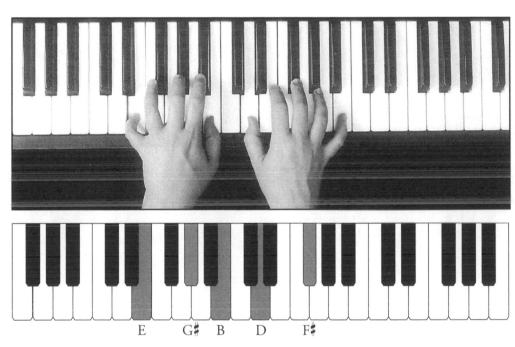

E   G♯   B   D   F♯

E9sus4

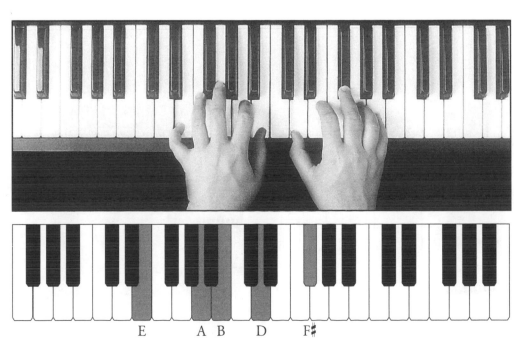

E   A B   D   F♯

E9♭5

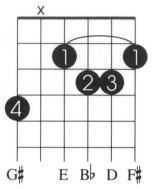

x

G# E B♭ D F#

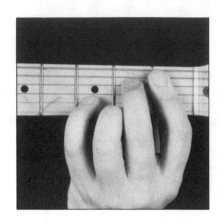
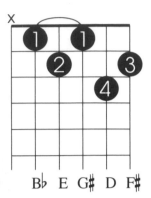

x

B♭ E G# D F#

E9♯5

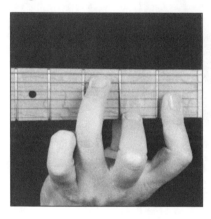
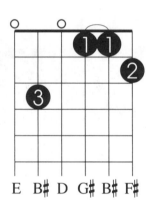

O   O

E B# D G# B# F#

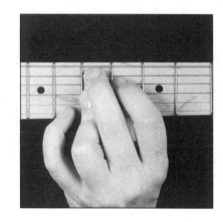
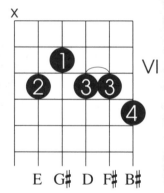

x

VI

E G# D F# B#

E13

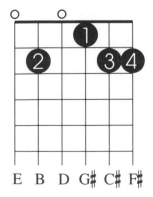

O   O

E B D G# C# F#

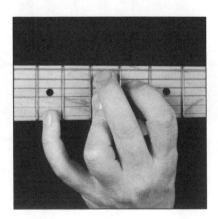
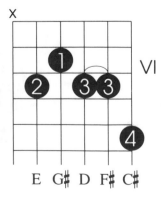

x

VI

E G# D F# C#

E9♭5

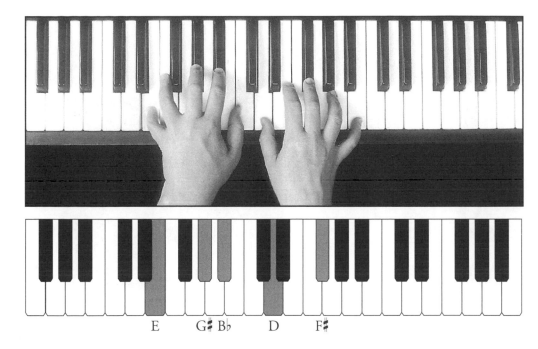

E G♯ B♭ D F♯

E9♯5

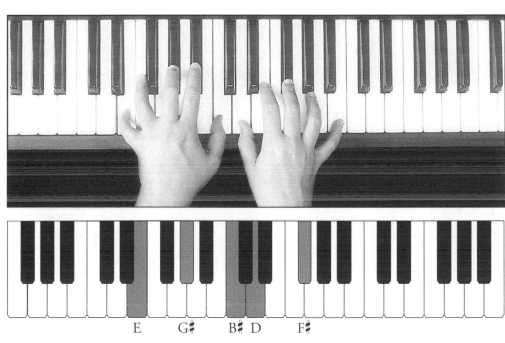

E G♯ B♯ D F♯

E13

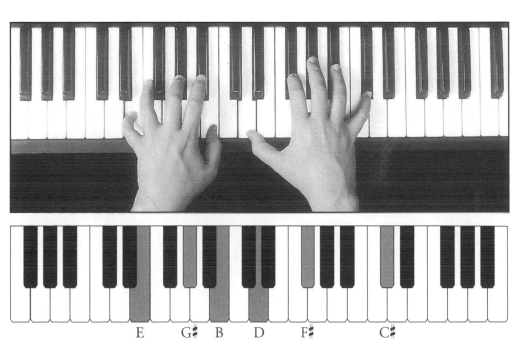

E G♯ B D F♯ C♯

E major9

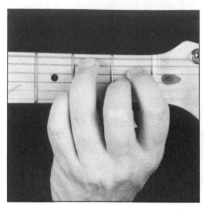 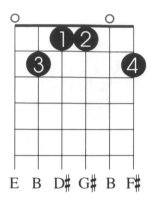

E B D# G# B F#

 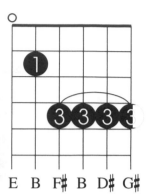

E B F# B D# G#

E major13

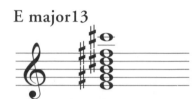

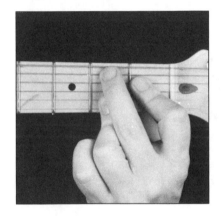 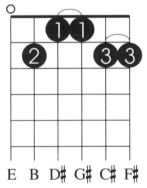

E B D# G# C# F#

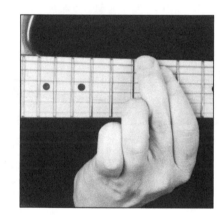 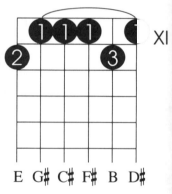

XI

E G# C# F# B D#

E minor9

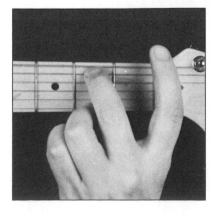 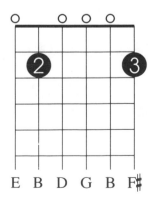

E B D G B F#

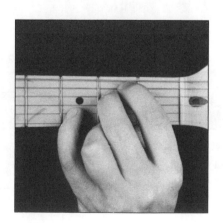 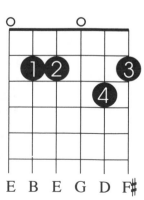

E B E G D F#

E major9

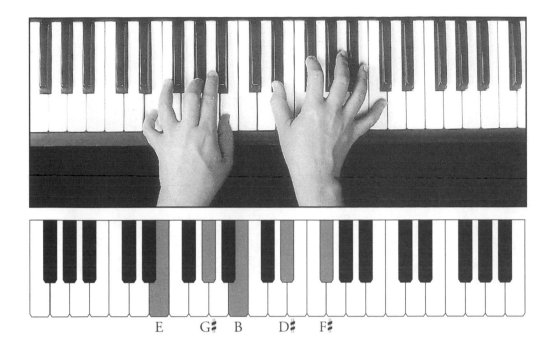

E   G♯   B   D♯   F♯

E major13

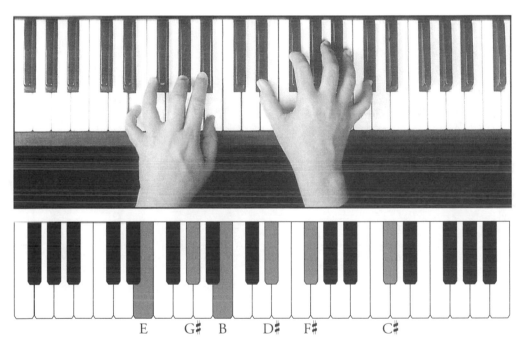

E   G♯ B   D♯ F♯   C♯

E minor9

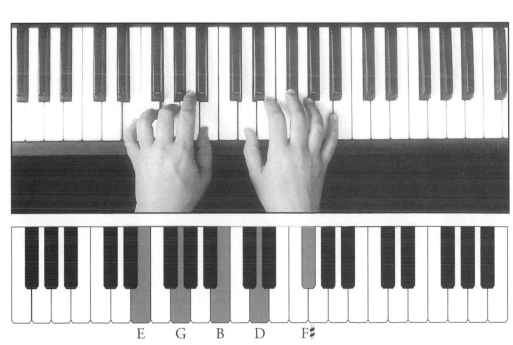

E   G   B   D   F♯

E minor11

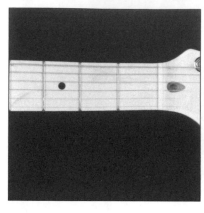

E A D G B E

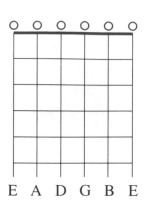

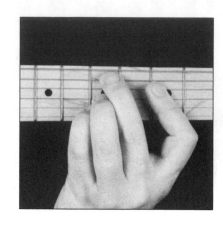

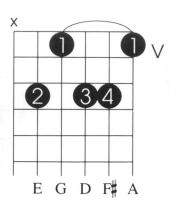

E G D F# A

E minor13

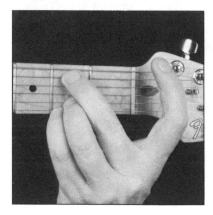

E B D G C# F#

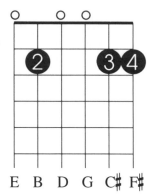

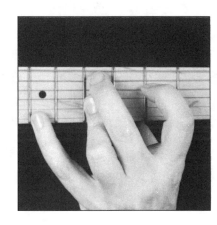

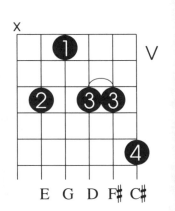

E G D F# C#

E minor11

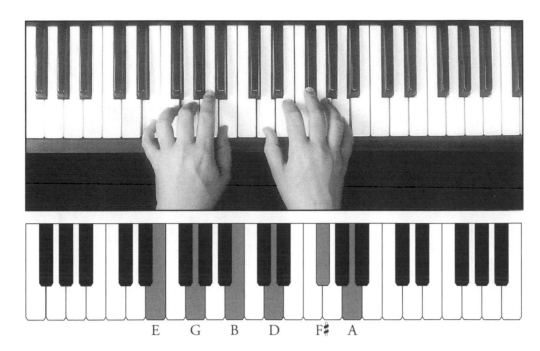

E minor13

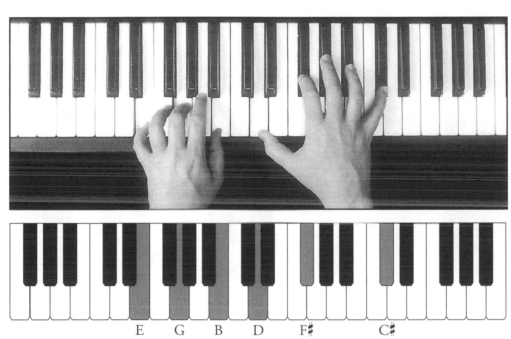

F Chords

F major

 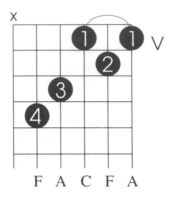

F A C F A   V

 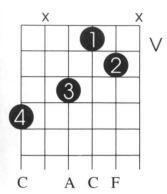

C A C F   V

Fsus4

 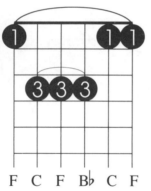

F C F B♭ C F

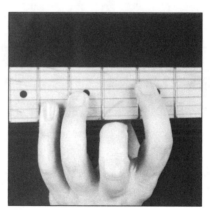 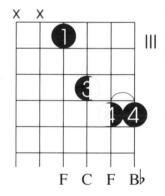

F C F B♭   III

F6

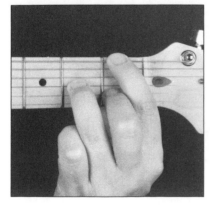 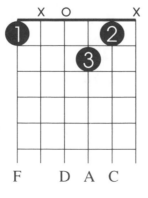

F D A C

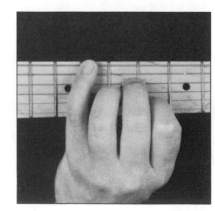 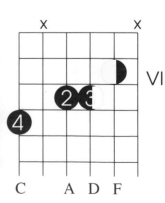

C A D F   VI

F major

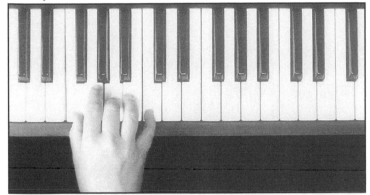

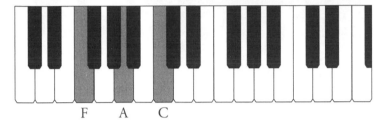

F   A   C

F major *first inversion*

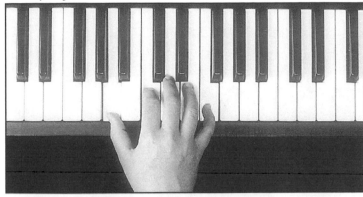

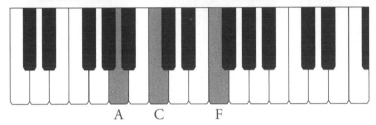

A   C   F

Fsus4

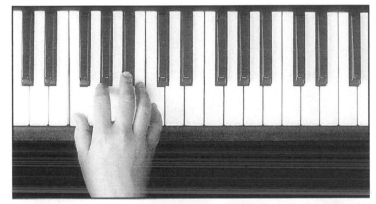

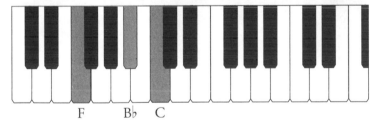

F   B♭ C

Fsus4 *first inversion*

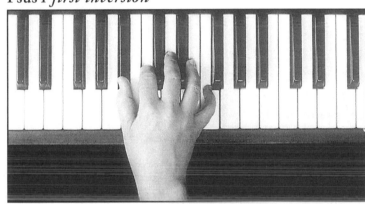

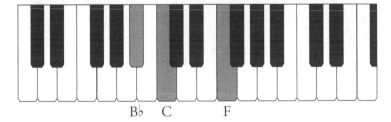

B♭ C   F

F6

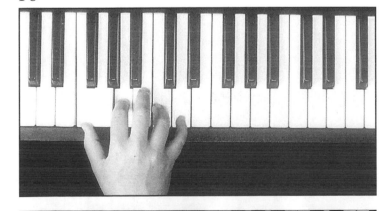

F   A   C D

F6 *first inversion*

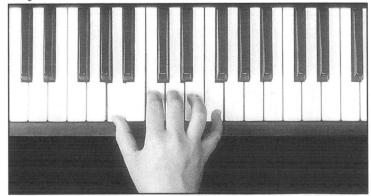

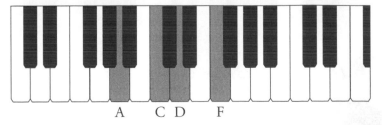

A   C D   F

F7

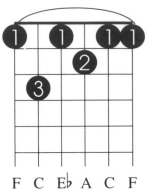

F C E♭ A C F

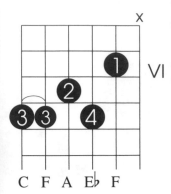

C F A E♭ F

VI

F°7

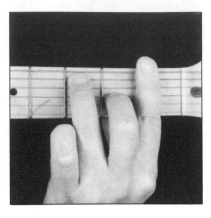

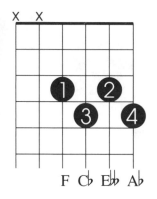

F C♭ E♭♭ A♭

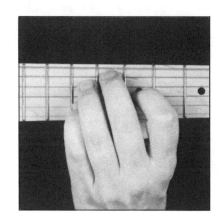

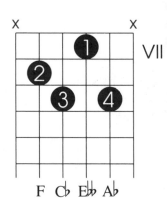

F C♭ E♭♭ A♭

VII

F major7

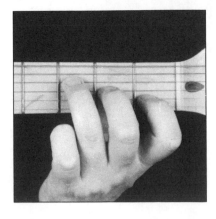

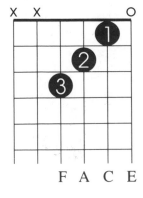

F A C E

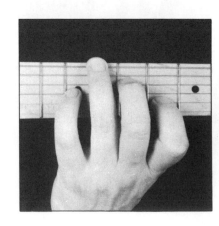

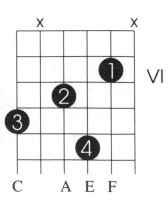

C A E F

VI

F7

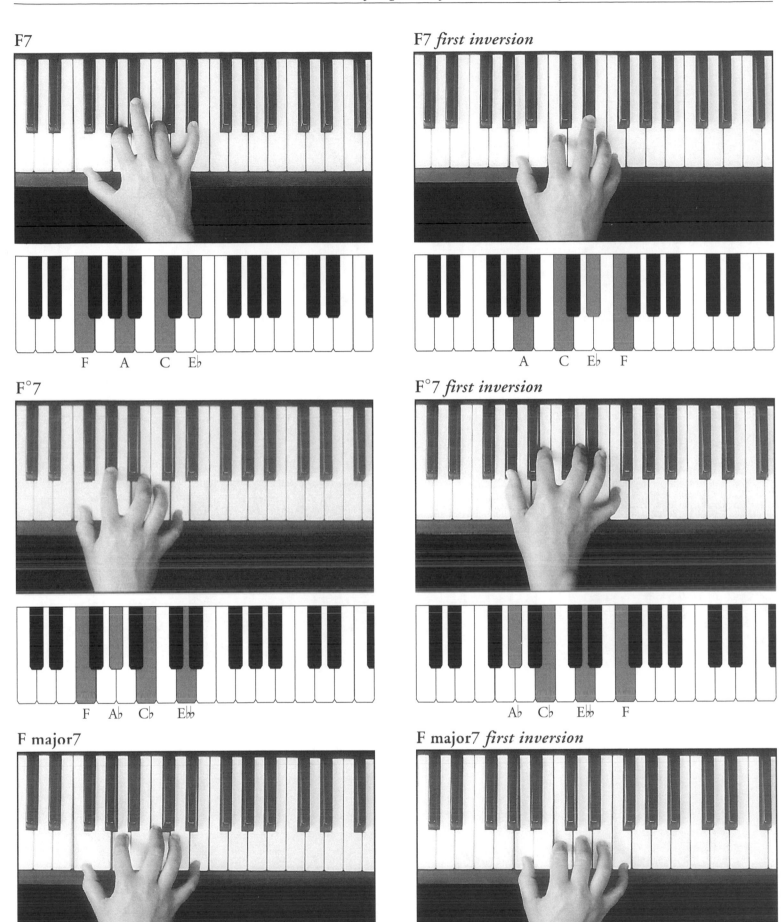

F A C E♭

F7 *first inversion*

A C E♭ F

F°7

F A♭ C♭ E♭♭

F°7 *first inversion*

A♭ C♭ E♭♭ F

F major7

F A C E

F major7 *first inversion*

A C E F

F minor

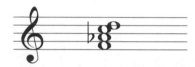

F C F A♭ C F

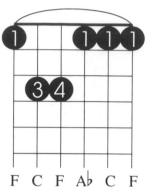
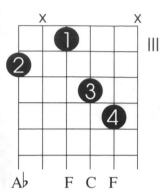

A♭ F C F

F minor6

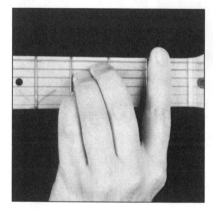
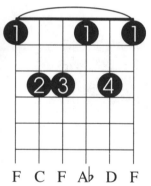

F C F A♭ D F

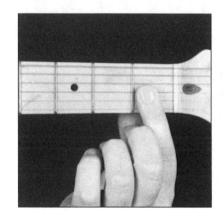
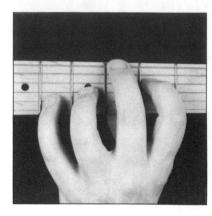

D A♭ C F

F minor7

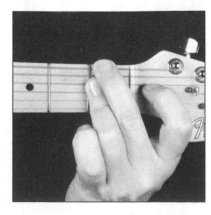
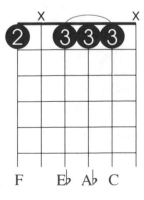

F E♭ A♭ C

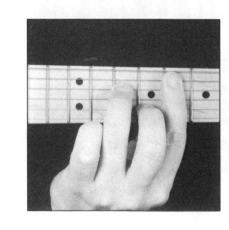
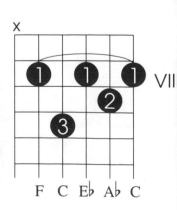

F C E♭ A♭ C

F minor

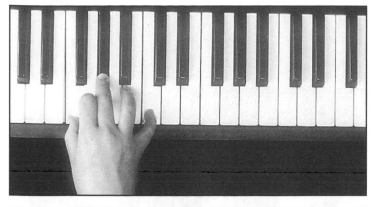

F A♭ C

F minor *first inversion*

A♭ C F

F minor6

F A♭ C D

F minor6 *first inversion*

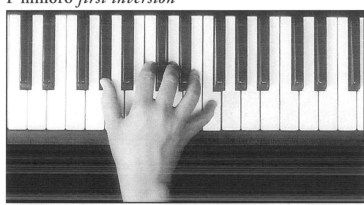

A♭ C D F

F minor7

F A♭ C E♭

F minor7 *first inversion*

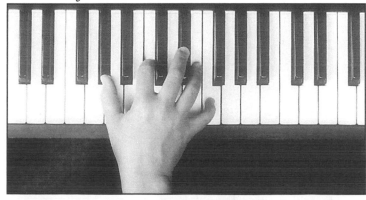

A♭ C E♭ F

F minor7♭5

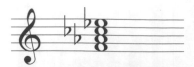

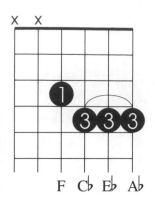

x x

F C♭ E♭ A♭

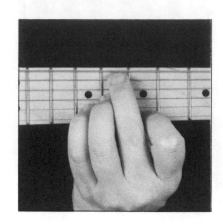
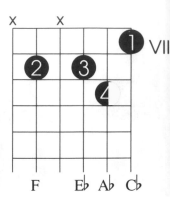

x   x

VII

F E♭ A♭ C♭

F minor (major7)

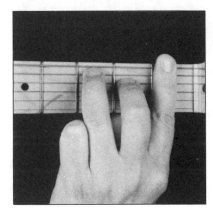
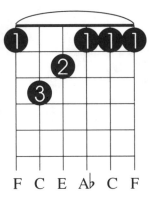

F C E A♭ C F

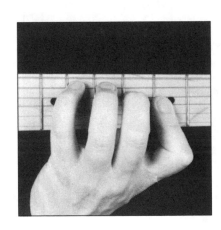
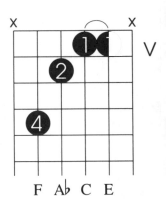

x   x

V

F A♭ C E

F minor7♭5

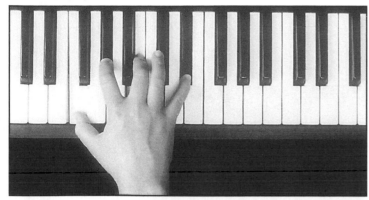

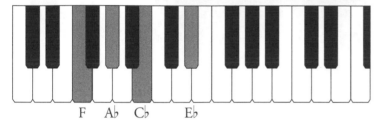

F   A♭   C♭   E♭

F minor7♭5 *first inversion*

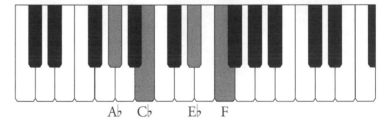

A♭   C♭   E♭   F

F minor (major7)

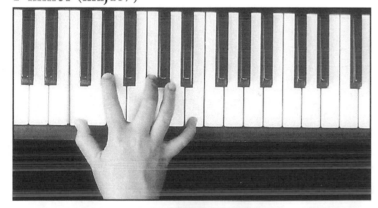

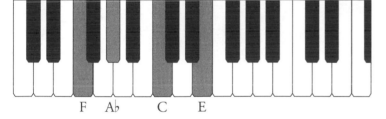

F   A♭   C   E

F minor (major7) *first inversion*

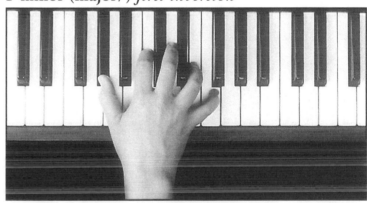

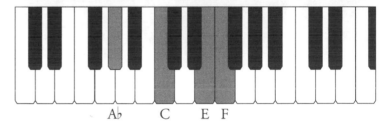

A♭   C   E   F

F6/9

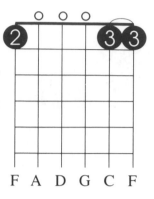

F A D G C F

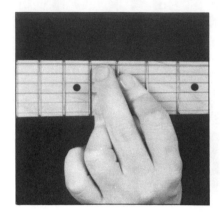
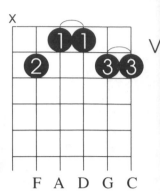

F A D G C

V

F9

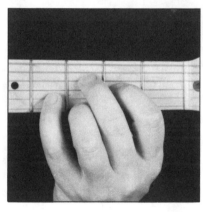
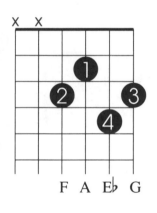

F A E♭ G

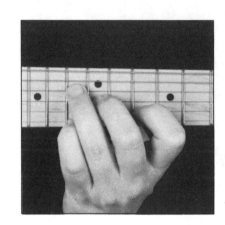
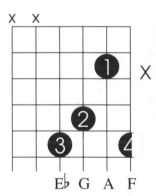

E♭ G A F

X

F9sus4

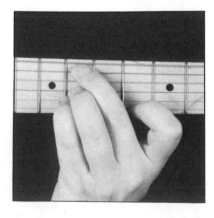

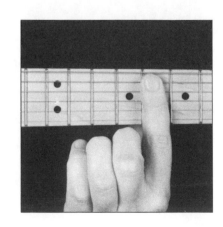
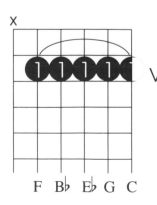

F B♭ E♭ G C

VI

F6/9

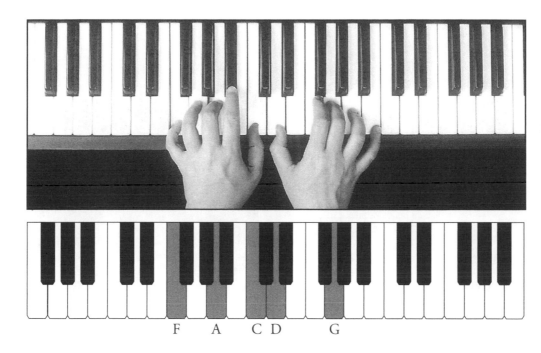

F A C D G

F9

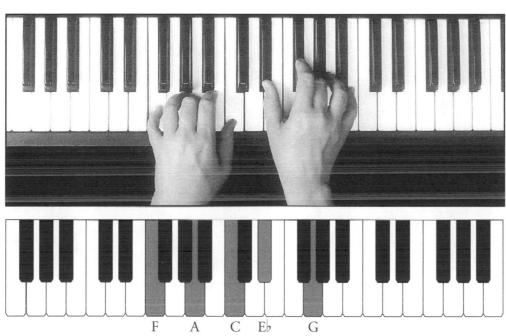

F A C E♭ G

F9sus4

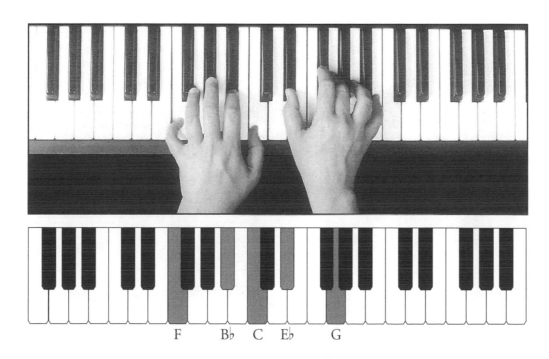

F B♭ C E♭ G

F9♭5

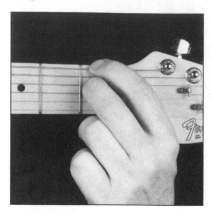

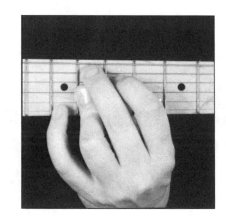

F A E♭ G C♭

F A E♭ G C♭ VI

F9♯5

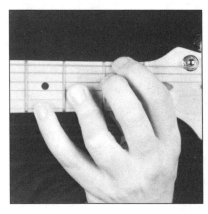

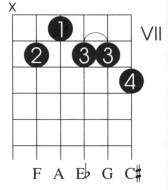

F E♭ A C♯ G

F A E♭ G C♯ VII

F13

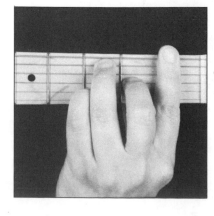

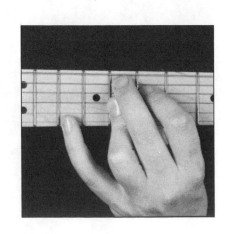

F C E♭ A D F

F A E♭ G D VII

F9♭5

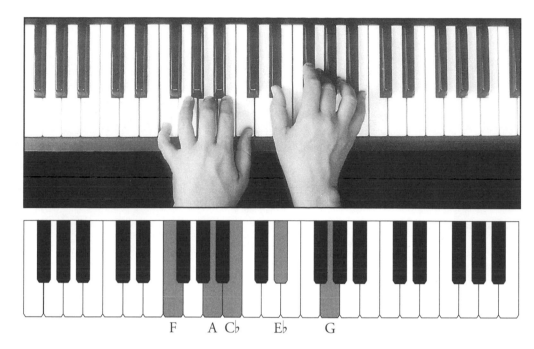

F A C♭ E♭ G

F9♯5

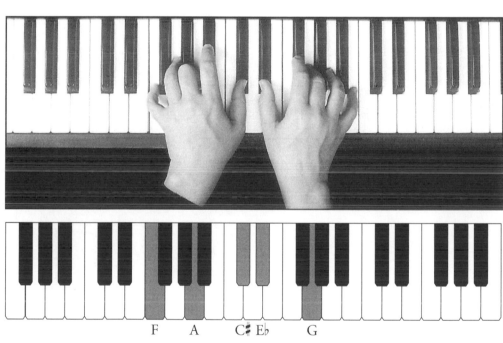

F A C♯ E♭ G

F13

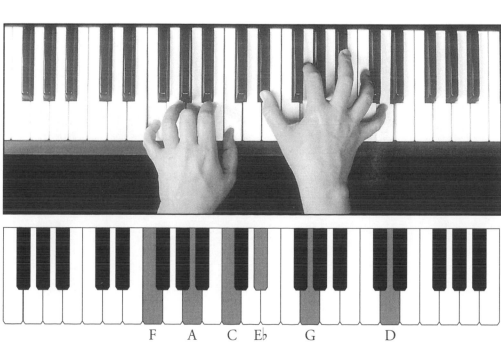

F A C E♭ G D

F major9

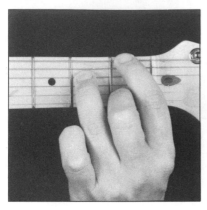
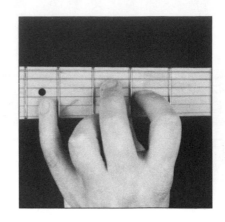

F A E G C

F A E G

F major13

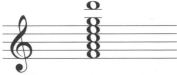

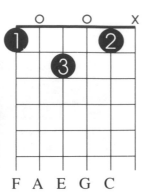
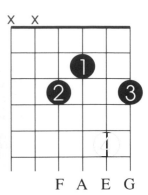

F E A D

F A D G C E

XII

F minor9

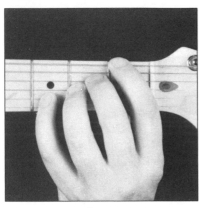
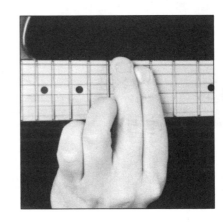

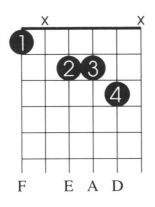
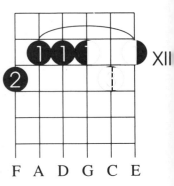

F A♭ E♭ G

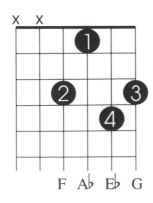
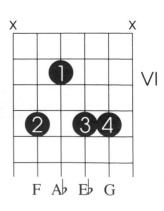

F A♭ E♭ G

VI

F major9

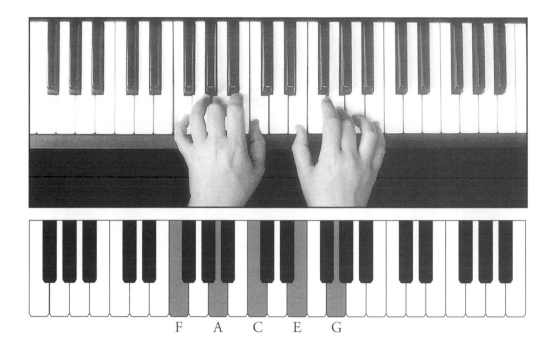

F A C E G

F major13

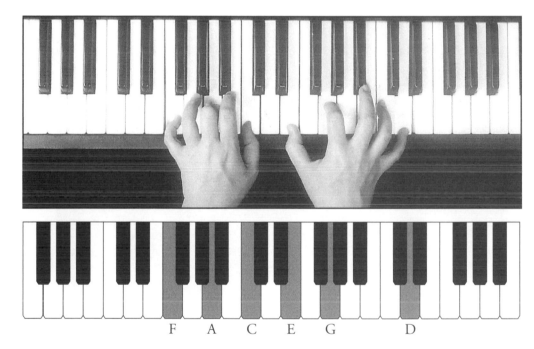

F A C E G D

F minor9

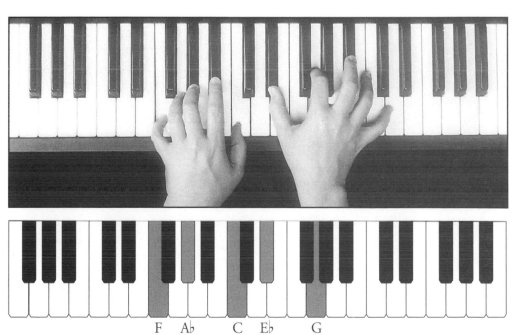

F A♭ C E♭ G

F minor11

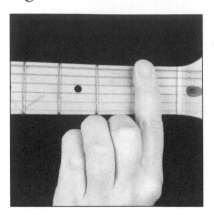

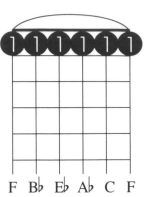

F B♭ E♭ A♭ C F

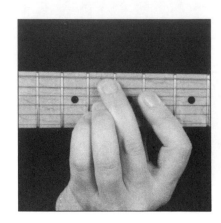

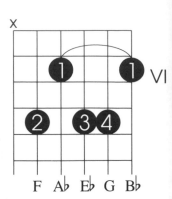

x

VI

F A♭ E♭ G B♭

F minor13

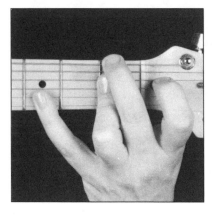

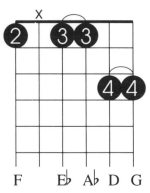

x

F E♭ A♭ D G

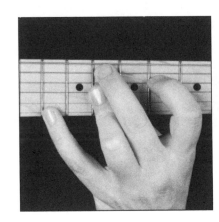

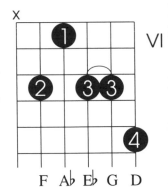

x

VI

F A♭ E♭ G D

F minor11

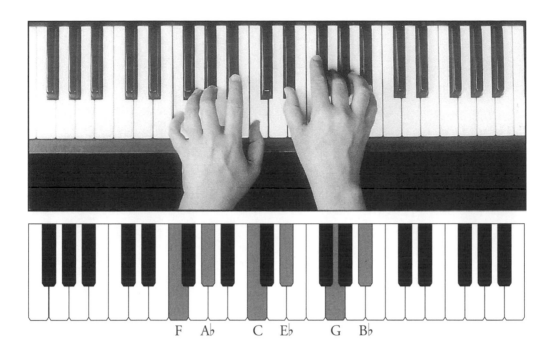

F Ab C Eb G Bb

F minor13

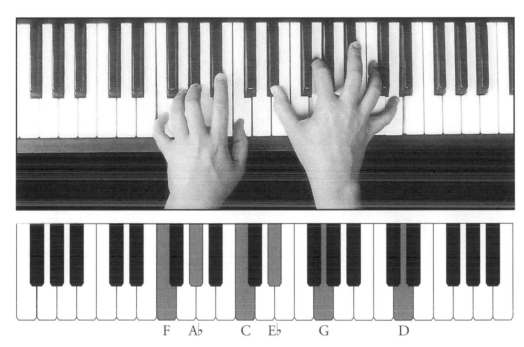

F Ab C Eb G D

F# Chords

F# major

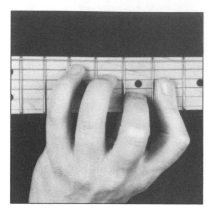

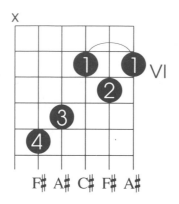

x
① ① VI
②
③
④

F# A# C# F# A#

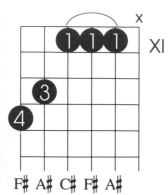

① ① ① XI
③
④

F# A# C# F# A#

F#sus4

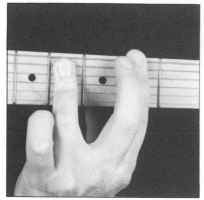

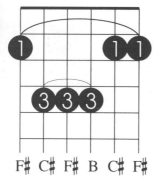

① ① ① ①
③ ③ ③

F# C# F# B C# F#

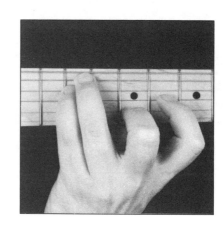

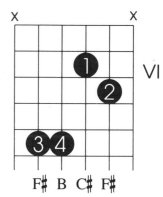

x   x
① VI
②
③ ④

F# B C# F#

F#6

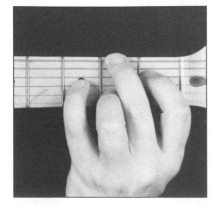

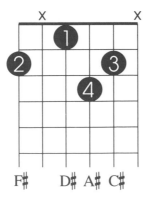

x   x
①
② ③
④

F#   D# A# C#

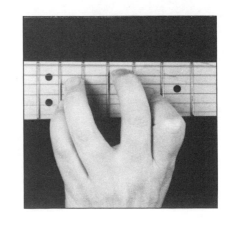

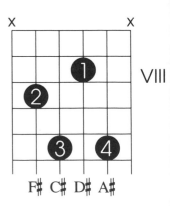

x   x
① VIII
②
③ ④

F# C# D# A#

F♯ major

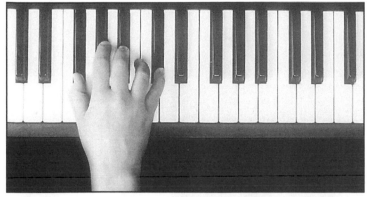

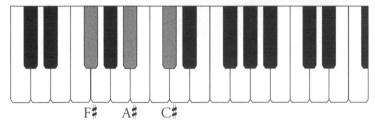

F♯   A♯   C♯

F♯ major *first inversion*

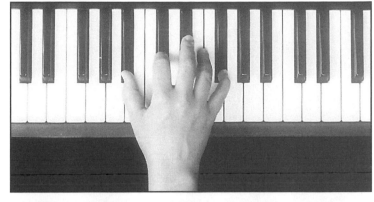

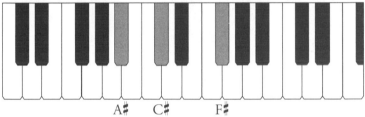

A♯   C♯   F♯

F♯sus4

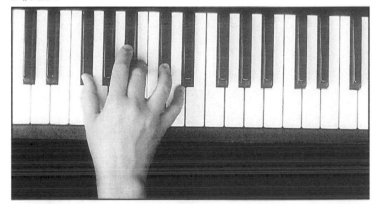

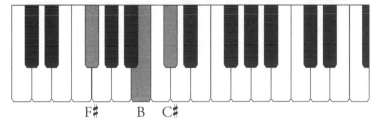

F♯   B   C♯

F♯sus4 *first inversion*

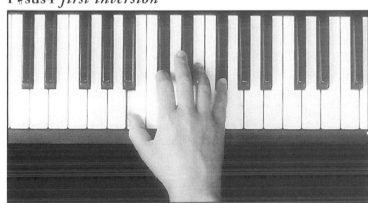

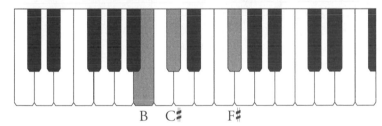

B   C♯   F♯

F♯6

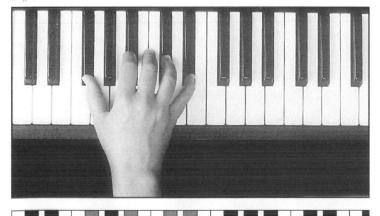

F♯   A♯   C♯ D♯

F♯6 *first inversion*

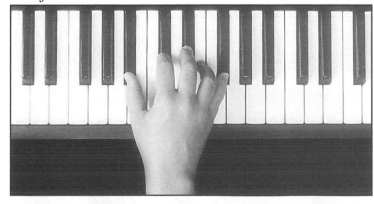

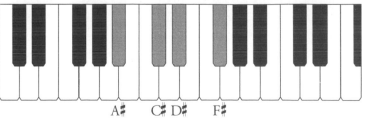

A♯   C♯ D♯   F♯

F#7

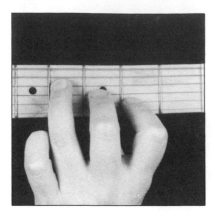

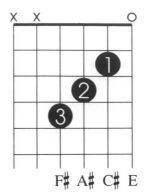

F# A# C# E

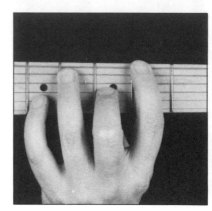

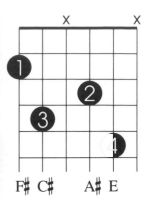

F# C# A# E

F#°7

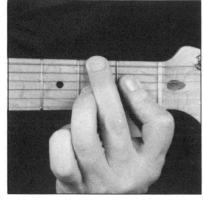

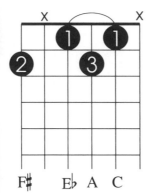

F# E♭ A C

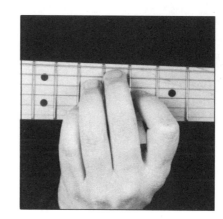

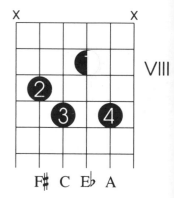

VIII

F# C E♭ A

F# major7

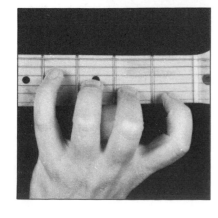

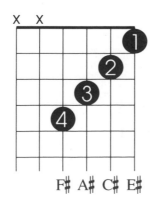

F# A# C# E#

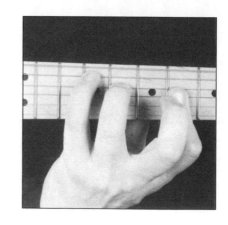

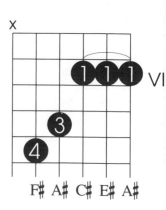

VI

F# A# C# E# A#

F♯7

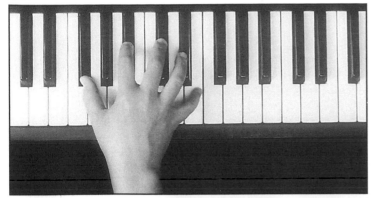

F♯ A♯ C♯ E

F♯7 *first inversion*

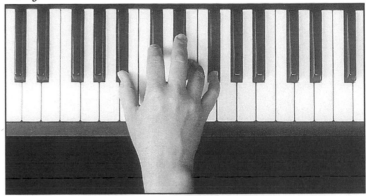

A♯ C♯ E F♯

F♯°7

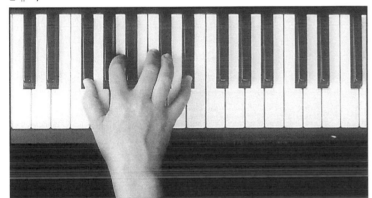

F♯ A C E♭

F♯°7 *first inversion*

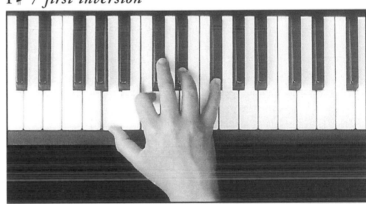

A C E♭ F♯

F♯ major7

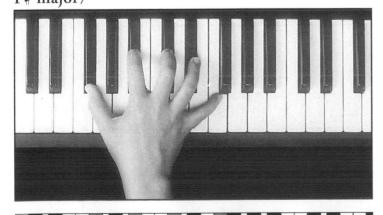

F♯ A♯ C♯ E♯

F♯ major7 *first inversion*

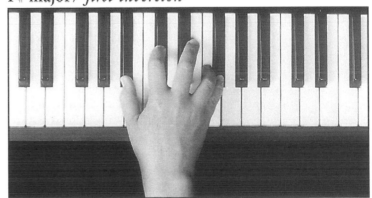

A♯ C♯ E♯ F♯

F# minor

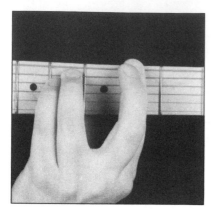
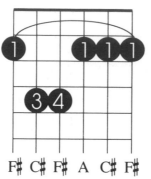

F# C# F# A C# F#

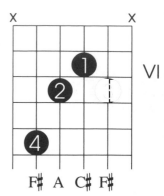

VI

F# A C# F#

F# minor6

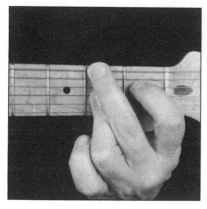
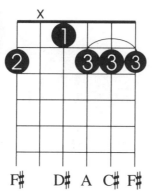

F# D# A C# F#

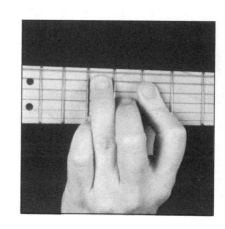

VII

F# A D# F# C#

F# minor7

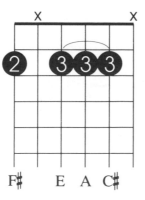

F# E A C#

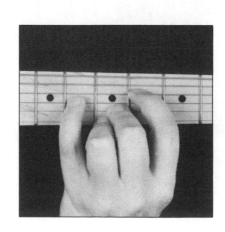

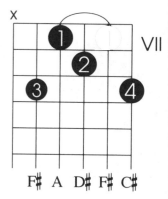

IV

F# C# E A

F# minor

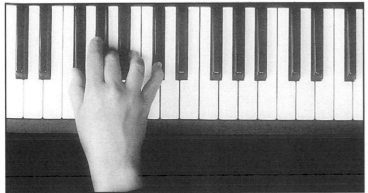

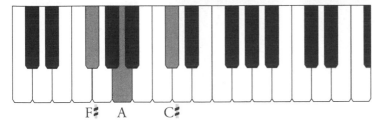

F# A   C#

F# minor *first inversion*

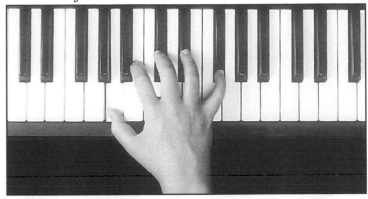

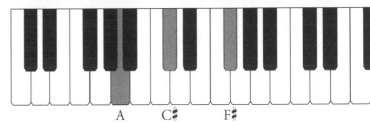

A   C#   F#

F# minor6

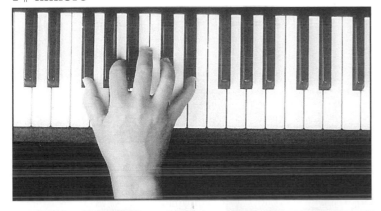

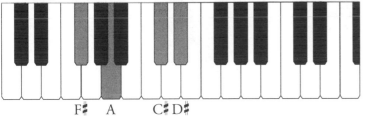

F# A   C#D#

F# minor6 *first inversion*

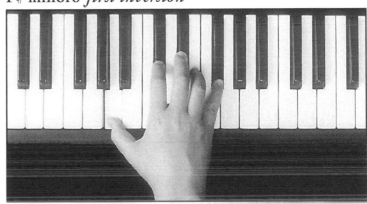

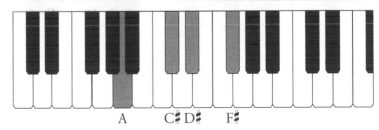

A   C#D#   F#

F# minor7

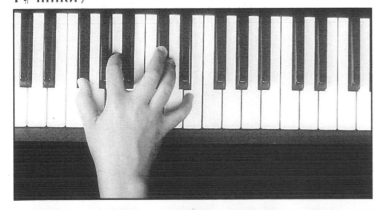

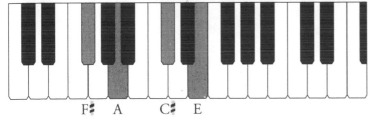

F# A   C# E

F# minor7 *first inversion*

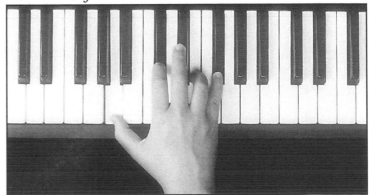

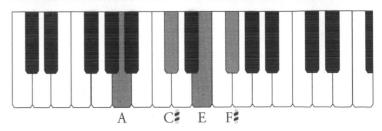

A   C# E F#

F# minor7♭5

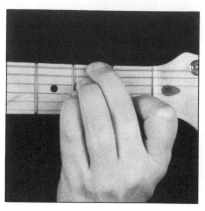
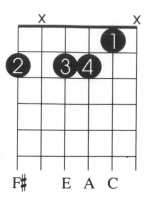

F#   E   A   C

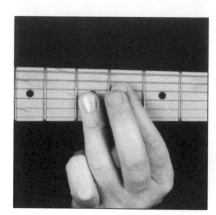
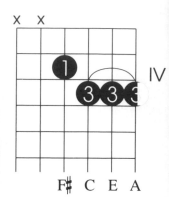

IV

F#   C   E   A

F# minor (major7)

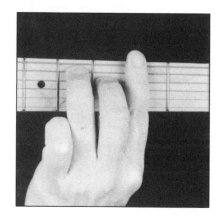
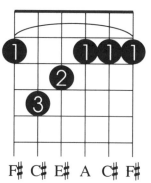

F# C# E# A C# F#

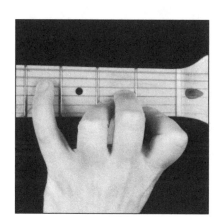
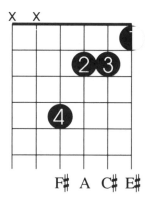

F#   A   C#   E#

F# minor7♭5

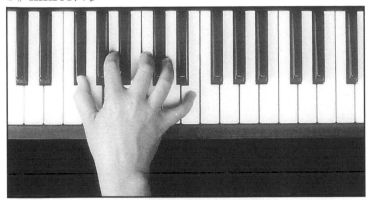

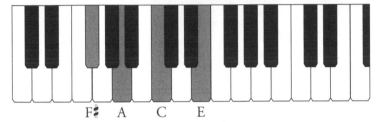

F#   A   C   E

F# minor7♭5 *first inversion*

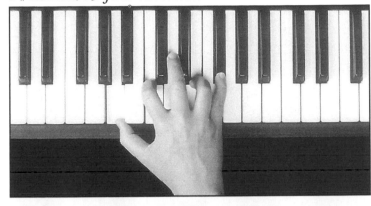

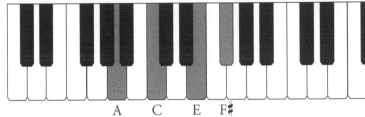

A   C   E   F#

F# minor (major7)

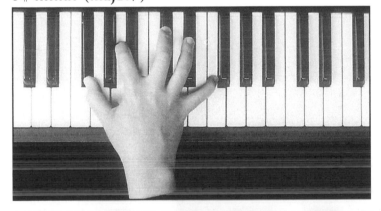

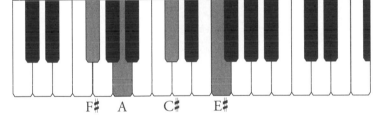

F#   A   C#   E#

F# minor (major7) *first inversion*

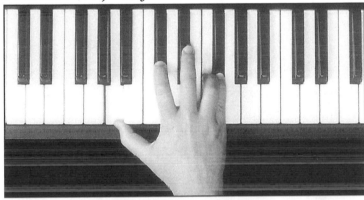

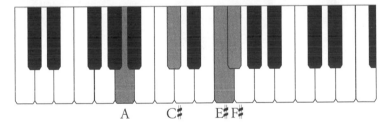

A   C#   E# F#

F#6/9

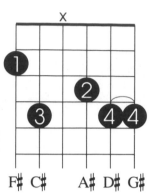

F# C# A# D# G#

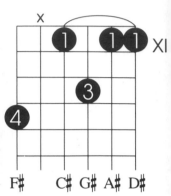

XI

F# C# G# A# D#

F#9

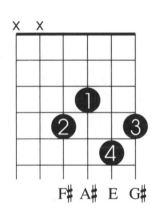

F# A# E G#

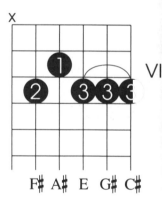

VI

F# A# E G# C#

F#9sus4

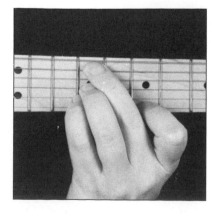

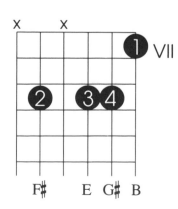

VII

F# E G# B

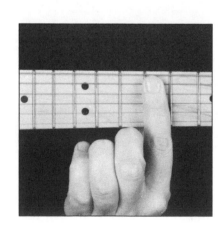

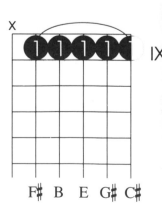

IX

F# B E G# C#

F♯6/9

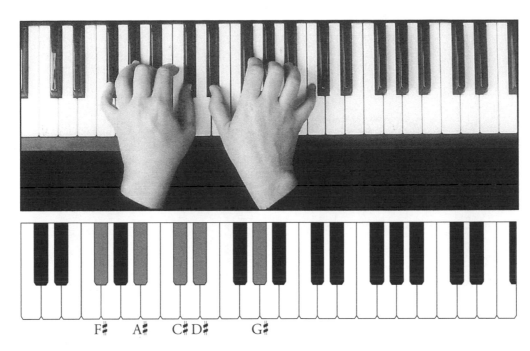

F♯   A♯   C♯ D♯   G♯

F♯9

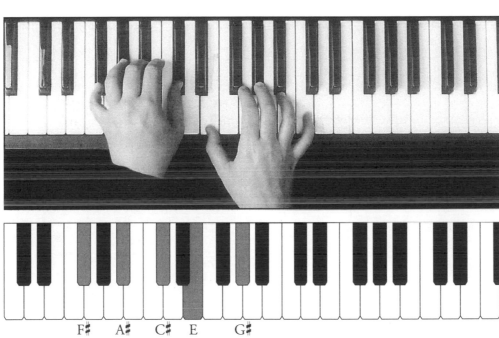

F♯   A♯   C♯   E   G♯

F♯9sus4

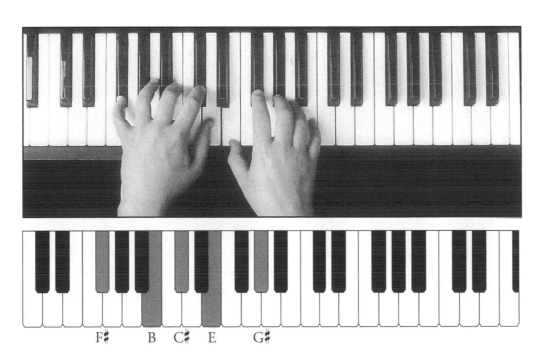

F♯   B   C♯   E   G♯

F♯9♭5

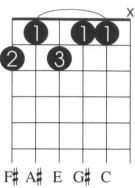

F♯ A♯ E G♯ C

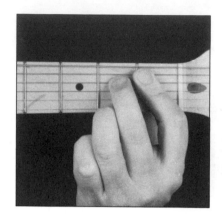
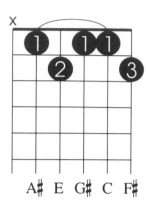

A♯ E G♯ C F♯

F♯9♯5

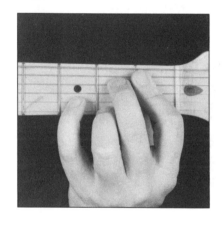
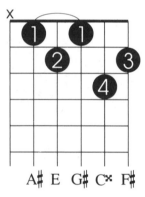

A♯ E G♯ C✕ F♯

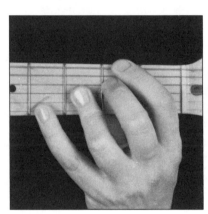
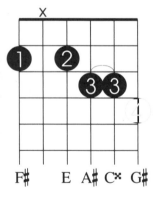

F♯ E A♯ C✕ G♯

F♯13

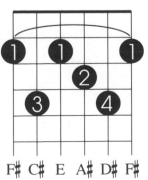

F♯ C♯ E A♯ D♯ F♯

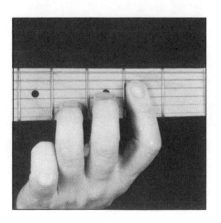
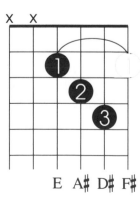

E A♯ D♯ F♯

F♯9♭5

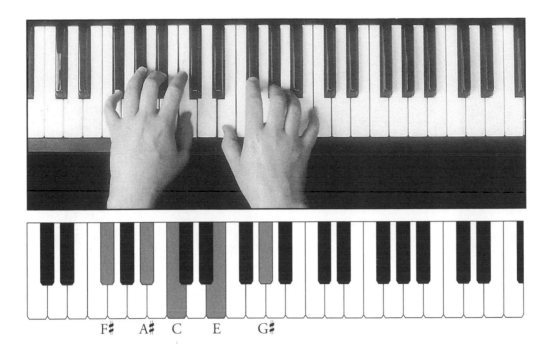

F♯   A♯   C   E   G♯

F♯9♯5

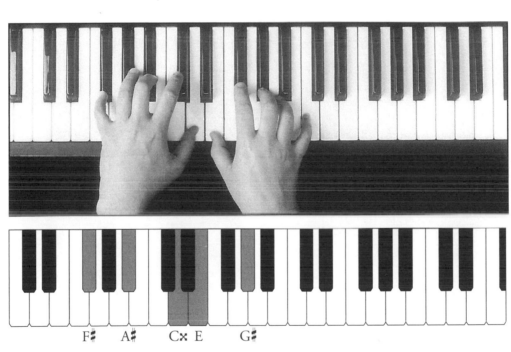

F♯   A♯   C✕ E   G♯

F♯13

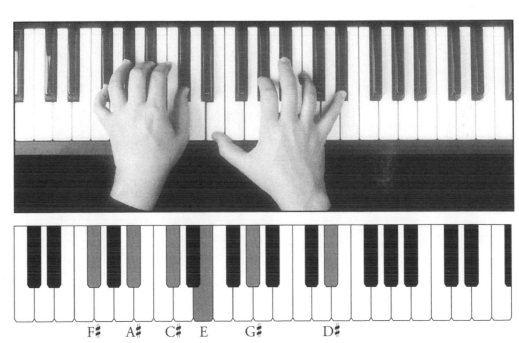

F♯   A♯   C♯   E   G♯   D♯

F# major9

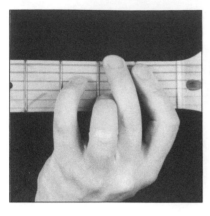

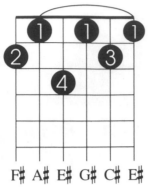

F# A# E# G# C# E#

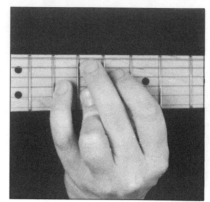

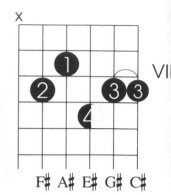

VI

F# A# E# G# C#

F# major13

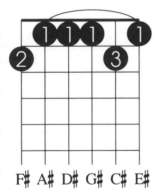

F# A# D# G# C# E#

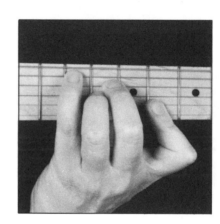

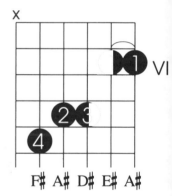

VI

F# A# D# E# A#

F# minor9

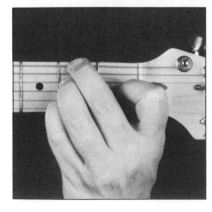

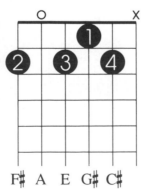

F# A E G# C#

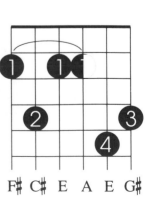

F# C# E A E G#

F♯ major9

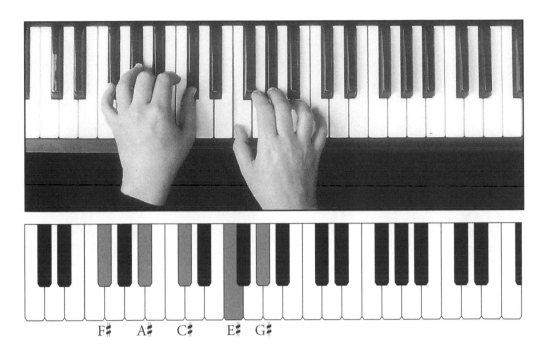

F♯   A♯   C♯   E♯ G♯

F♯ major13

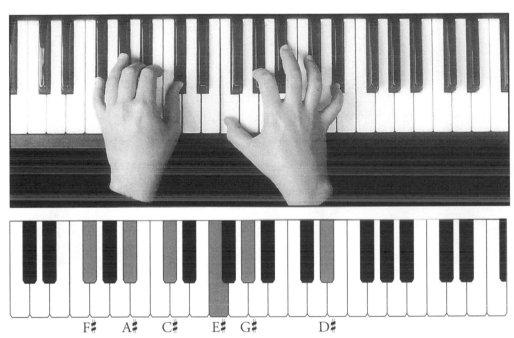

F♯   A♯   C♯   E♯ G♯   D♯

F♯ minor9

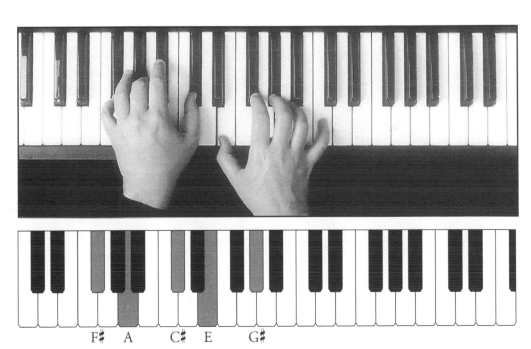

F♯   A   C♯   E   G♯

F♯ minor11

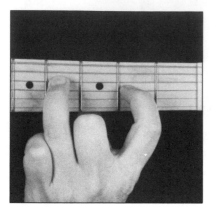

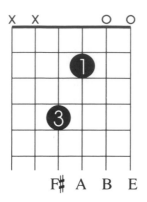

F♯ A B E

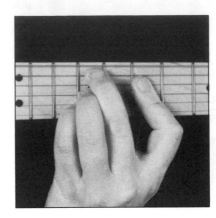

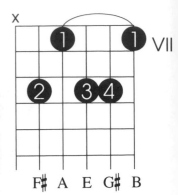

VII

F♯ A E G♯ B

F♯ minor13

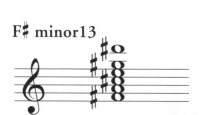

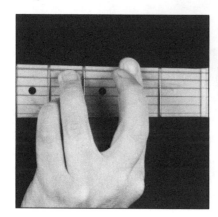

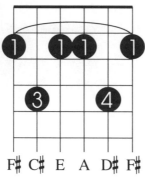

F♯ C♯ E A D♯ F♯

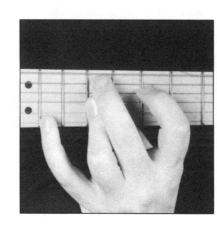

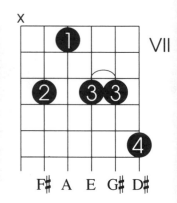

VII

F♯ A E G♯ D♯

F♯ minor11

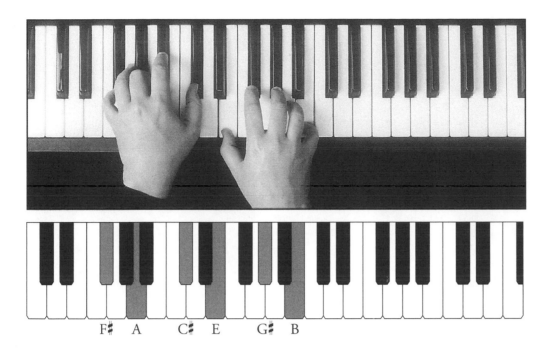

F♯   A   C♯   E   G♯   B

F♯ minor13

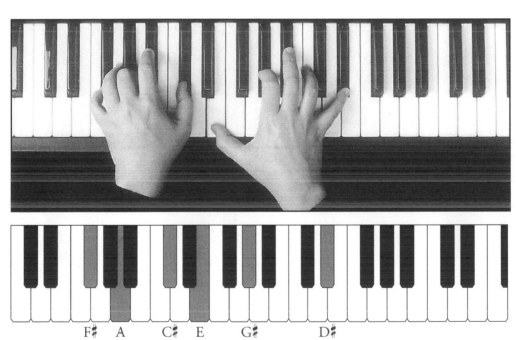

F♯   A   C♯   E   G♯   D♯

G Chords

G major

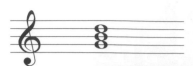

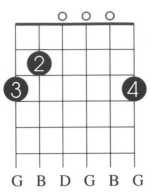

G B D G B G

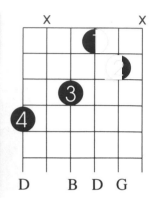

V

D B D G

Gsus4

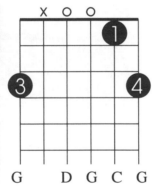

G D G C G

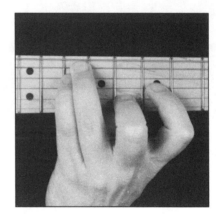

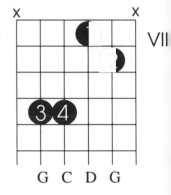

VII

G C D G

G6

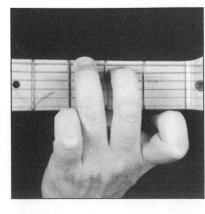

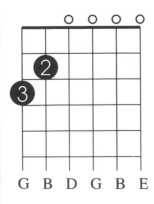

G B D G B E

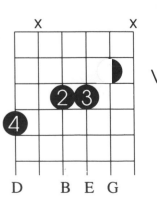

V

D B E G

126

G major

G   B   D

G major *first inversion*

B   D   G

Gsus4

G   C D

Gsus4 *first inversion*

C D   G

G6

G   B   D E

G6 *first inversion*

B   D E   G

G7

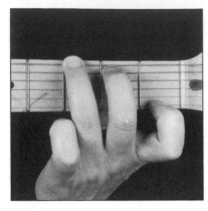
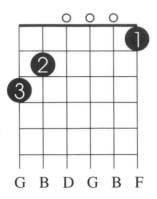

G B D G B F

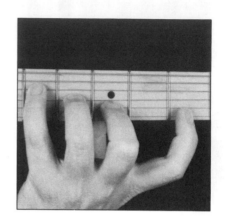
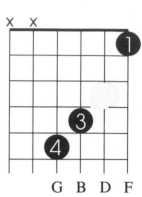

G B D F

G°7

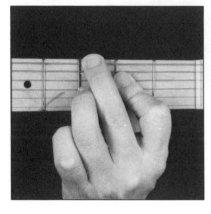
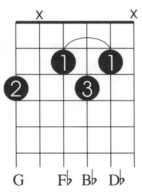

G F♭ B♭ D♭

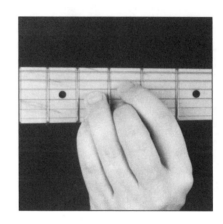
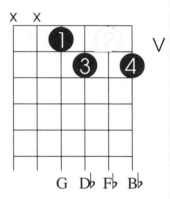

V

G D♭ F♭ B♭

G major7

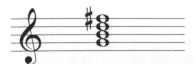

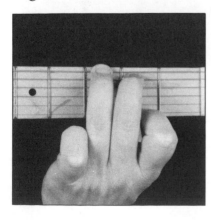
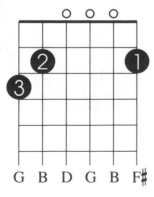

G B D G B F♯

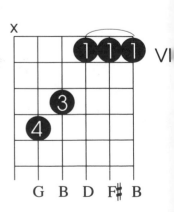

VI

G B D F♯ B

G7

G   B   D   F

G7 *first inversion*

B   D   F   G

G°7

G   B♭   D♭   F♭

G°7 *first inversion*

B♭   D♭   F♭   G

G major7

G   B   D   F♯

G major7 *first inversion*

B   D   F♯ G

G minor

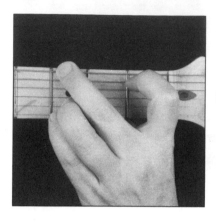

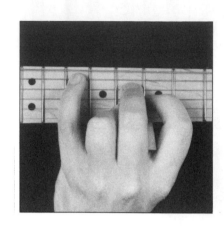

G Bb D G D G

G Bb D G

VII

G minor6

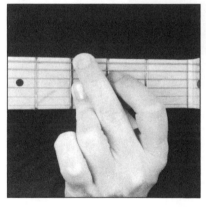

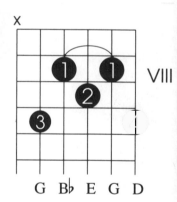

G E Bb D

G Bb E G D

VIII

G minor7

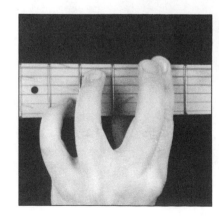

G F Bb D

G D F Bb F G

III

G minor

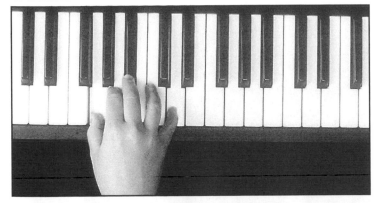

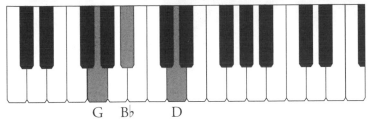

G   B♭   D

G minor *first inversion*

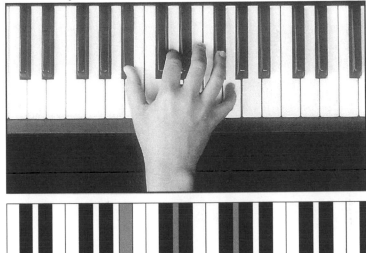

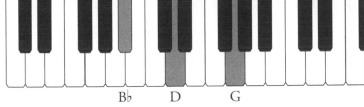

B♭   D   G

G minor6

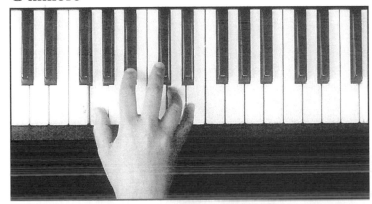

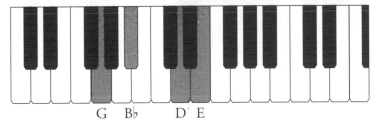

G   B♭   D E

G minor6 *first inversion*

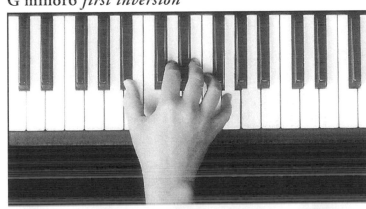

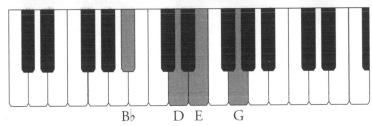

B♭   D E   G

G minor7

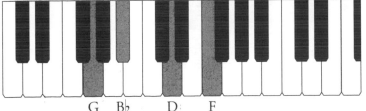

G   B♭   D   F

G minor7 *first inversion*

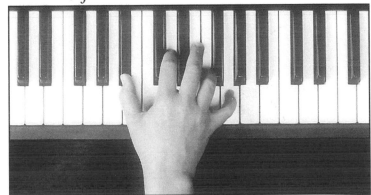

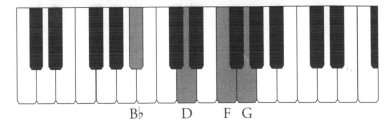

B♭   D   F G

G minor7♭5

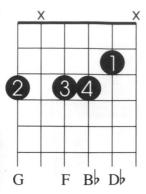

G F B♭ D♭

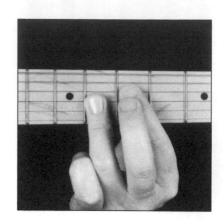

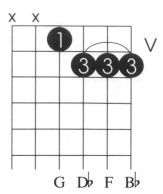

V

G D♭ F B♭

G minor (major7)

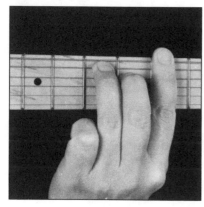

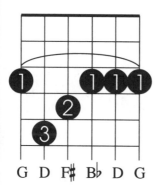

G D F♯ B♭ D G

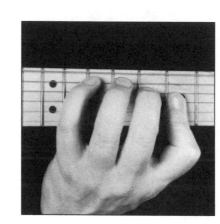

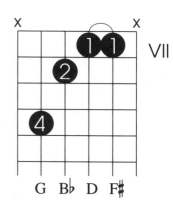

VII

G B♭ D F♯

G minor7♭5

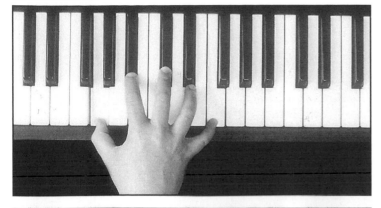

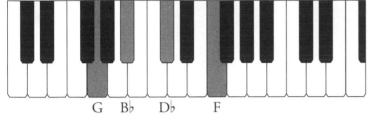

G B♭ D♭ F

G minor7♭5 *first inversion*

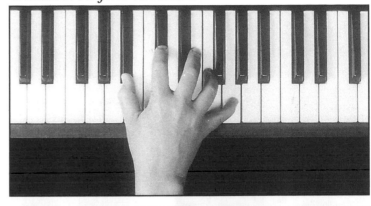

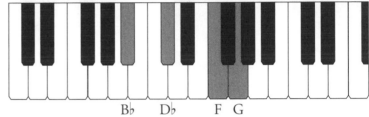

B♭ D♭ F G

G minor (major7)

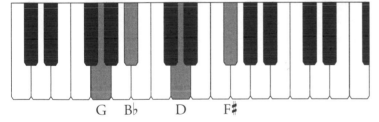

G B♭ D F♯

G minor (major7) *first inversion*

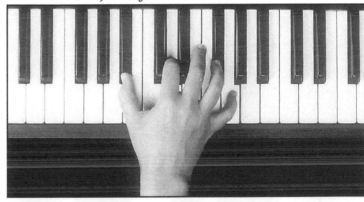

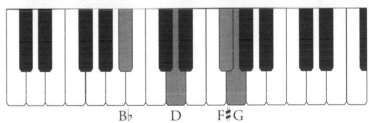

B♭ D F♯ G

G6/9

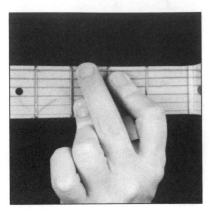 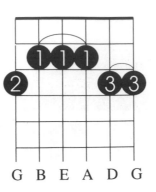

G B E A D G

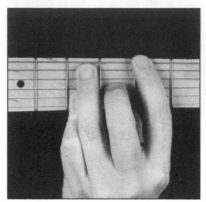 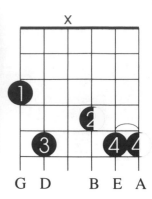

G D B E A

G9

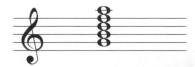

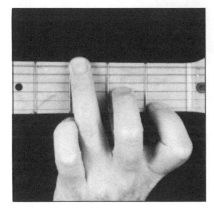 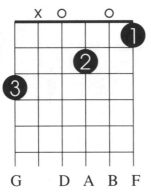

G D A B F

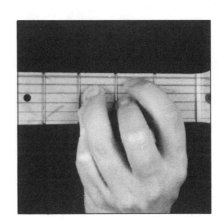 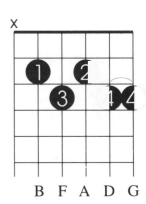

B F A D G

G9sus4

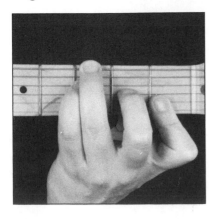 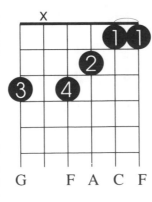

G F A C F

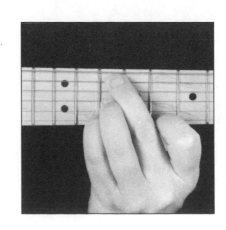 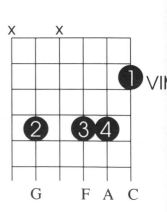

VII

G F A C

G6/9

G B D E A

G9

G B D F A

G9sus4

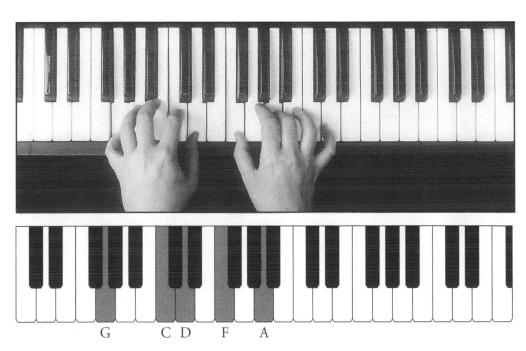

G C D F A

G9♭5

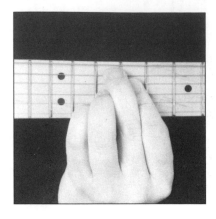
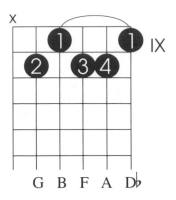
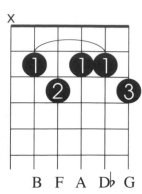

G9♯5

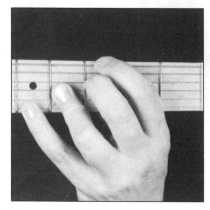
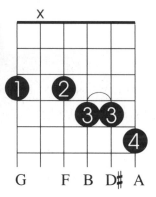
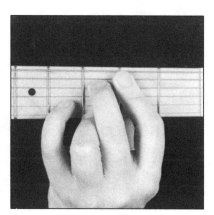
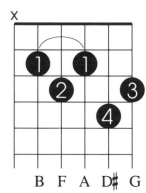

G13

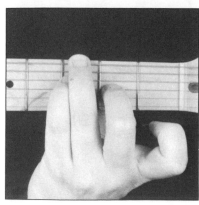
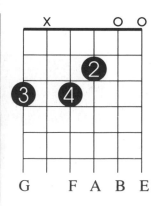

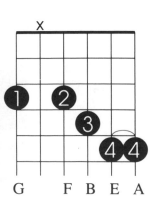

G9♭5

G B D♭ F A

G9♯5

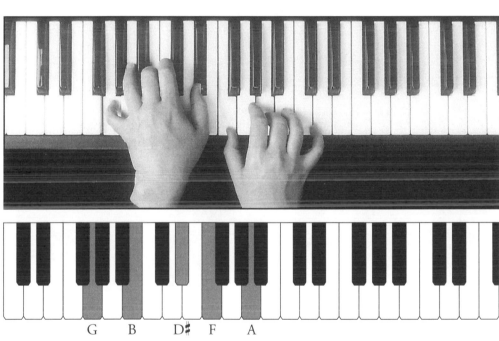

G B D♯ F A

G13

G B D F A E

G major9

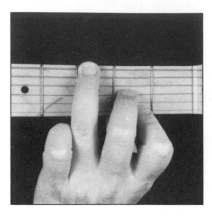

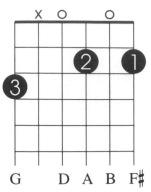

G   D A B F#

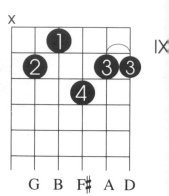

IX

G B F# A D

G major13

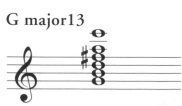

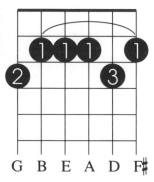

G B E A D F#

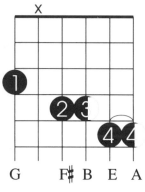

G   F# B E A

G minor9

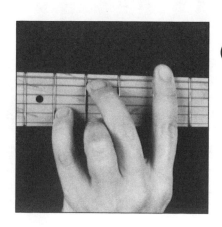

G   F Bb D A

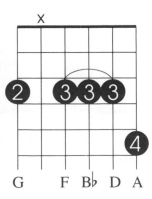

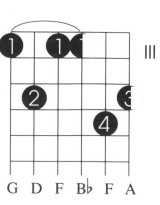

III

G D F Bb F A

G major9

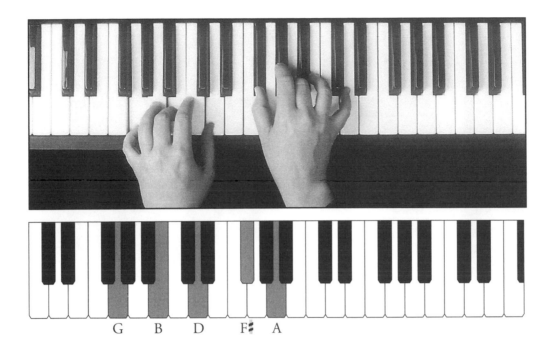

G B D F♯ A

G major13

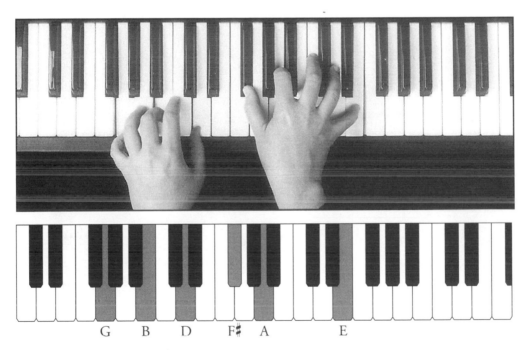

G B D F♯ A E

G minor9

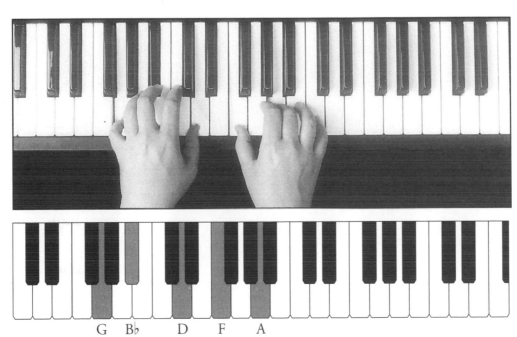

G B♭ D F A

G minor11

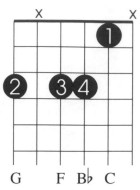

G   F B♭ C

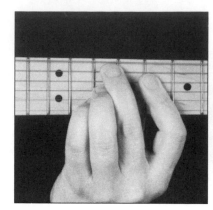

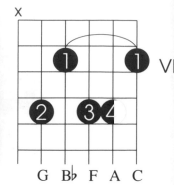

VI

G B♭ F A C

G minor13

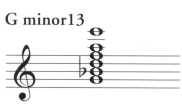

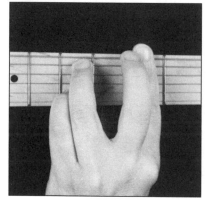

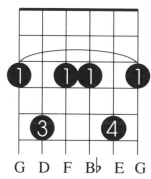

G D F B♭ E G

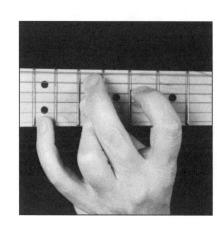

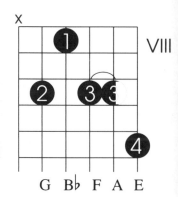

VIII

G B♭ F A E

G minor11

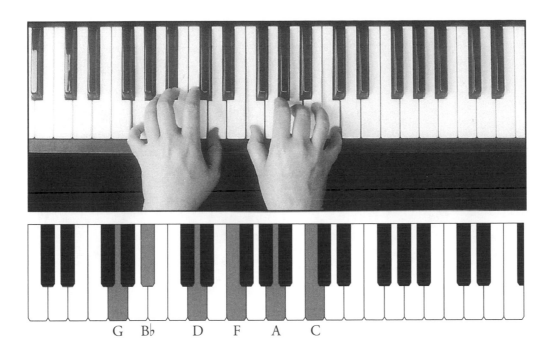

G B♭ D F A C

G minor13

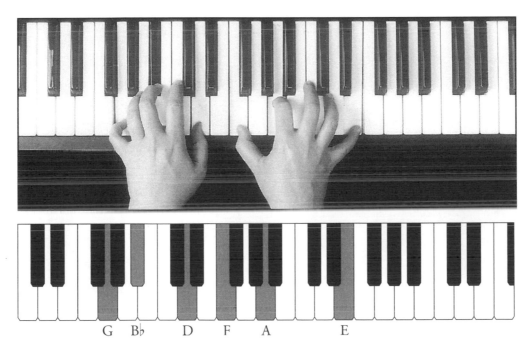

G B♭ D F A E

Ab Chords

Ab major

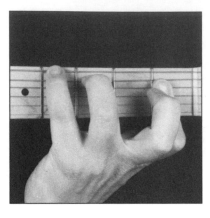

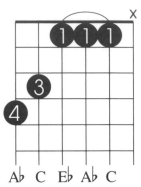

Ab C Eb Ab C

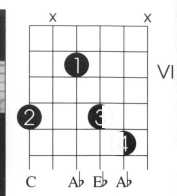

VI

C Ab Eb Ab

Absus4

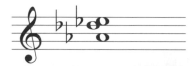

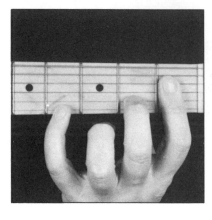

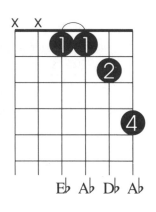

Eb Ab Db Ab

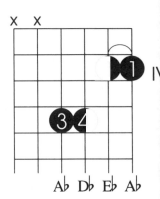

IV

Ab Db Eb Ab

Ab6

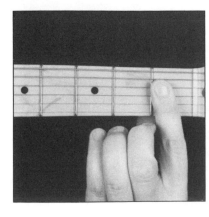

Eb Ab C F

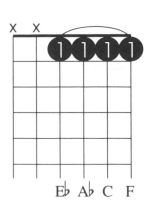

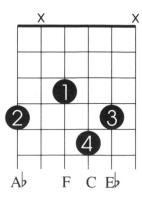

Ab F C Eb

A♭ major

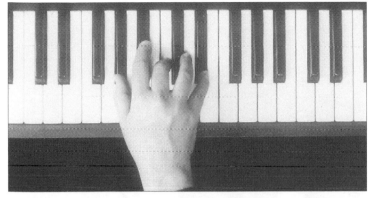

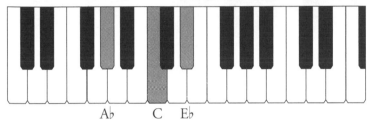

A♭   C E♭

A♭ major *first inversion*

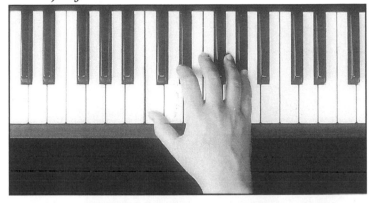

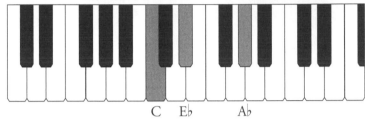

C E♭   A♭

A♭sus4

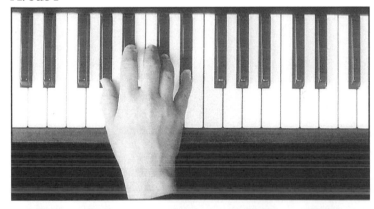

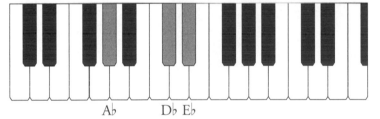

A♭   D♭ E♭

A♭sus4 *first inversion*

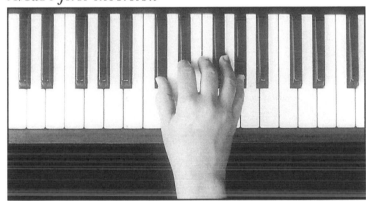

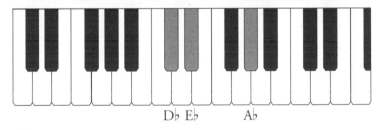

D♭ E♭   A♭

A♭6

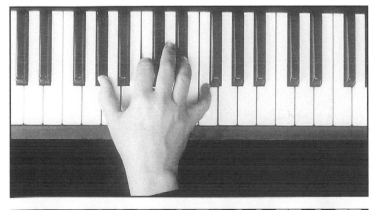

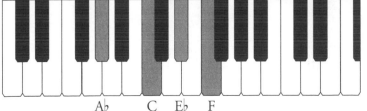

A♭   C E♭ F

A♭6 *first inversion*

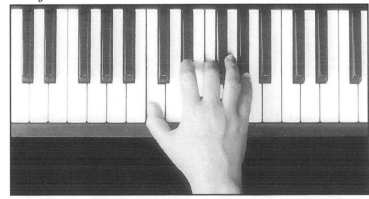

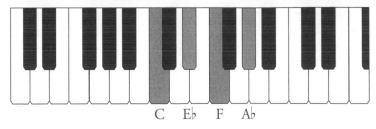

C E♭ F A♭

A♭7

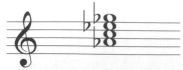

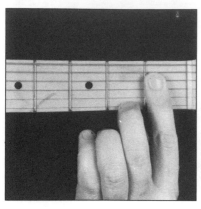

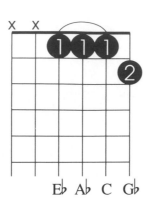

Eb Ab C Gb

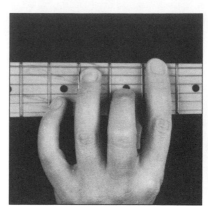

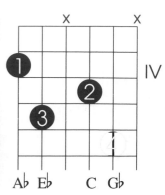

IV

Ab Eb C Gb

A♭°7

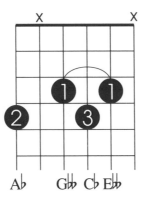

Ab Gbb Cb Ebb

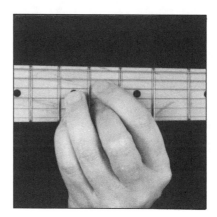

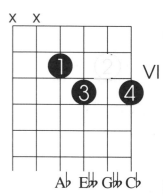

VI

Ab Ebb Gbb Cb

A♭ major7

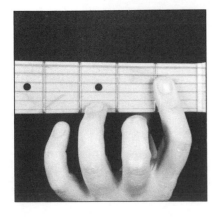

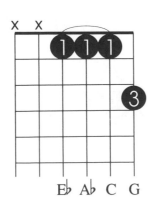

Eb Ab C G

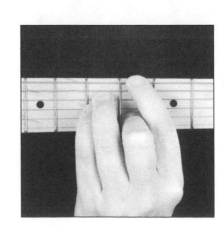

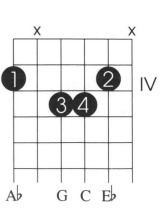

IV

Ab G C Eb

A♭7

A♭ C E♭ G♭

A♭7 *first inversion*

C E♭ G♭ A♭

A♭°7

A♭ C♭ E♭♭ G♭♭

A♭°7 *first inversion*

C♭ E♭♭ G♭♭ A♭

A♭ major7

A♭ C E♭ G

A♭ major7 *first inversion*

C E♭ G A♭

A♭ minor

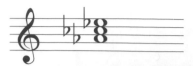

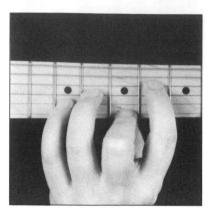

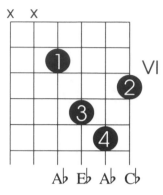

VI

Ab Eb Ab Cb

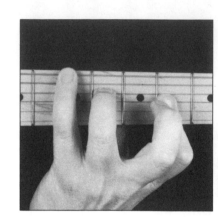

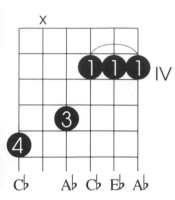

IV

Cb Ab Cb Eb Ab

A♭ minor6

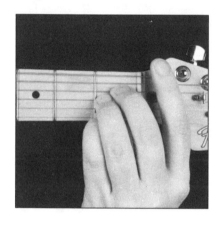

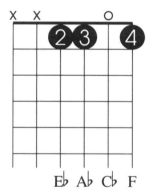

Eb Ab Cb F

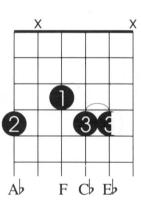

Ab F Cb Eb

A♭ minor7

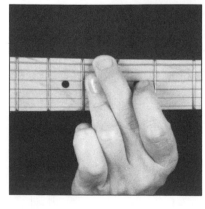

IV

Ab Gb Cb Eb

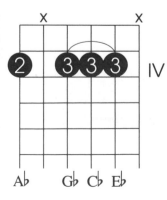

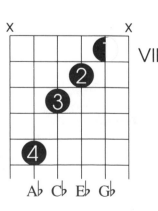

VII

Ab Cb Eb Gb

A♭ minor

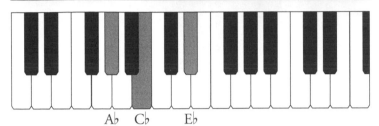

Ab   Cb   Eb

A♭ minor *first inversion*

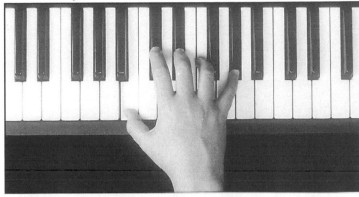

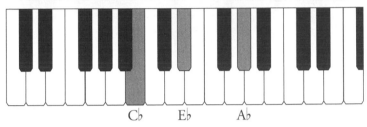

Cb   Eb   Ab

A♭ minor6

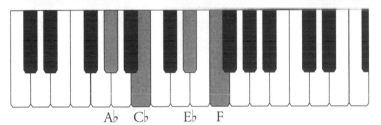

Ab   Cb   Eb   F

A♭ minor6 *first inversion*

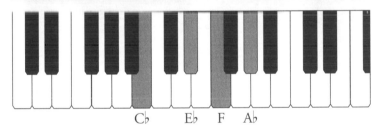

Cb   Eb   F   Ab

A♭ minor7

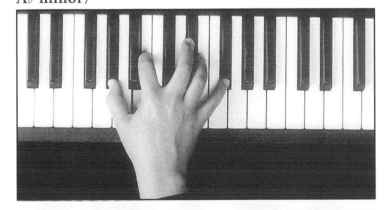

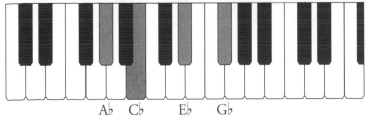

Ab   Cb   Eb   Gb

A♭ minor7 *first inversion*

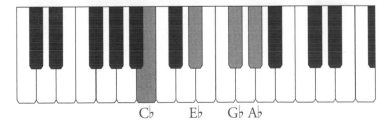

Cb   Eb   Gb Ab

Ab minor7b5

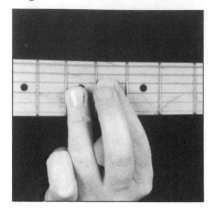

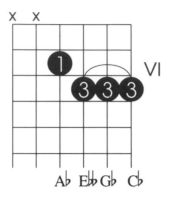

Ab Ebb Gb Cb — VI

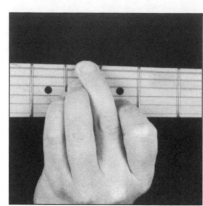

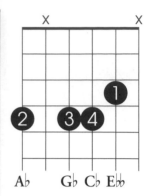

Ab Gb Cb Ebb

Ab minor (major7)

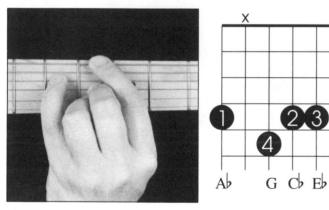

Ab G Cb Eb

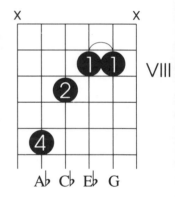

Ab Cb Eb G — VIII

A♭ minor7♭5

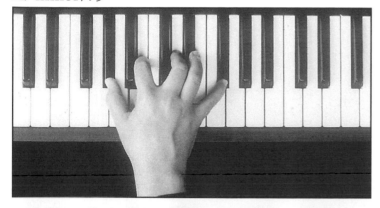

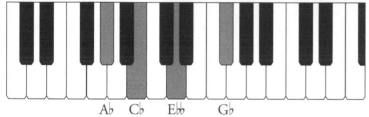

A♭ C♭ E♭♭ G♭

A♭ minor7♭5 *first inversion*

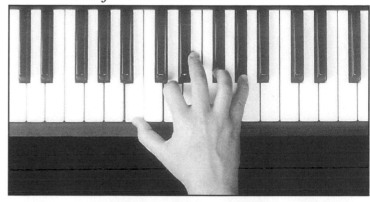

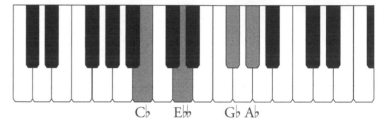

C♭ E♭♭ G♭ A♭

A♭ minor (major7)

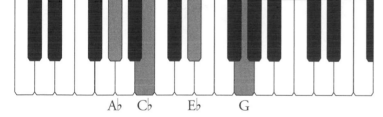

A♭ C♭ E♭ G

A♭ minor (major7) *first inversion*

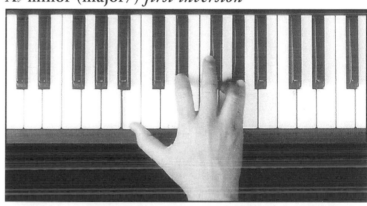

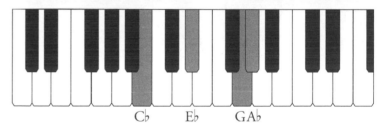

C♭ E♭ G A♭

A♭6/9

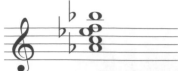

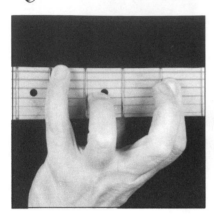

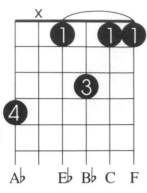

A♭ E♭ B♭ C F

C F B♭ E♭ A♭

A♭9

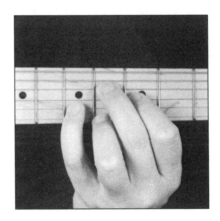

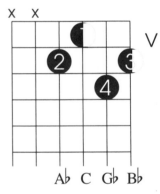

V

C G♭ B♭ E♭ A♭

A♭ C G♭ B♭

A♭9sus4

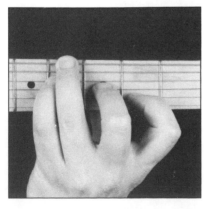

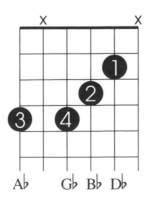

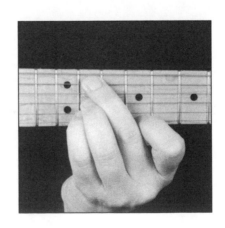

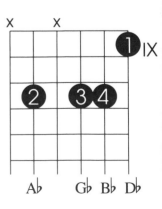

IX

A♭ G♭ B♭ D♭

A♭ G♭ B♭ D♭

A♭6/9

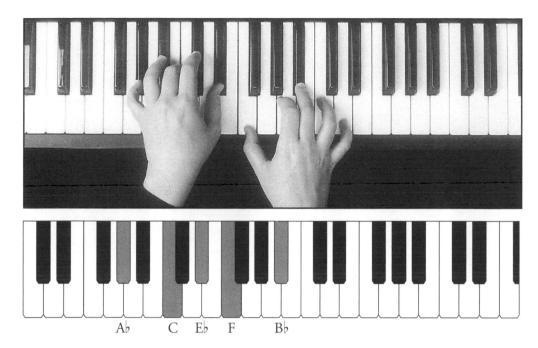

Ab   C   Eb   F   Bb

A♭9

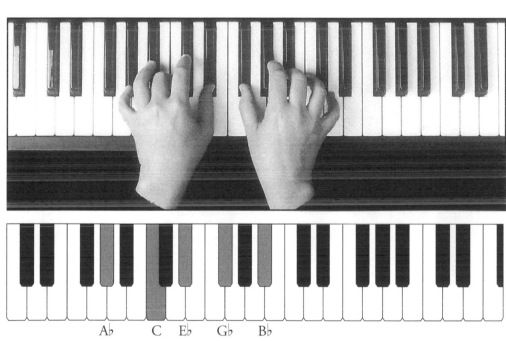

Ab   C   Eb   Gb   Bb

A♭9sus4

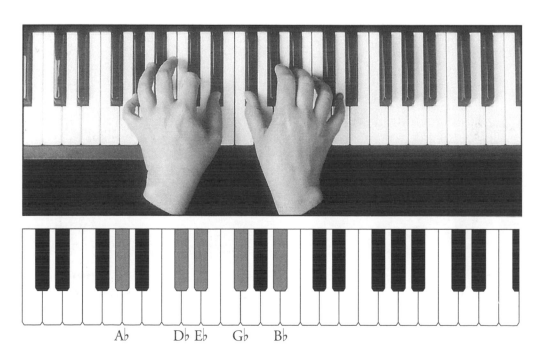

Ab   Db Eb   Gb   Bb

Ab9b5

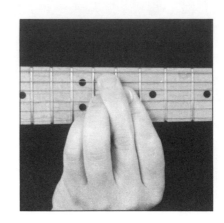

Ab C Gb Bb Ebb

Ab C Gb Bb Ebb

Ab9#5

Ab C Gb Bb E

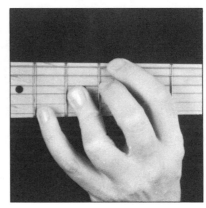

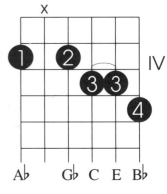

IV

Ab Gb C E Bb

Ab13

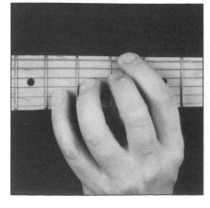

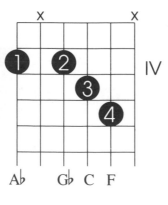

IV

Ab Gb C F

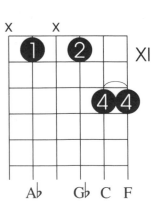

XI

Ab Gb C F

A♭9♭5

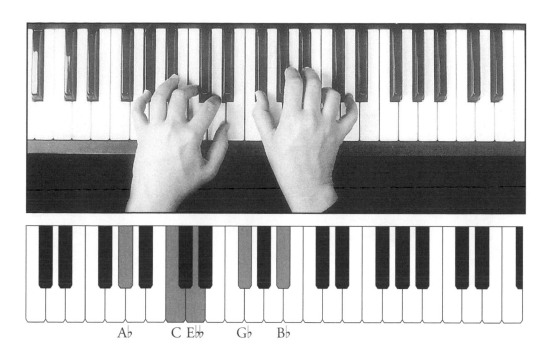

A♭   C E♭♭   G♭   B♭

A♭9♯5

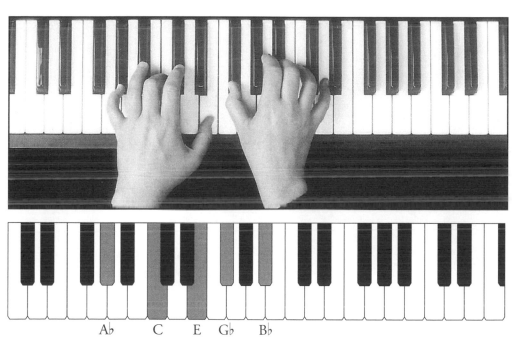

A♭   C   E   G♭   B♭

A♭13

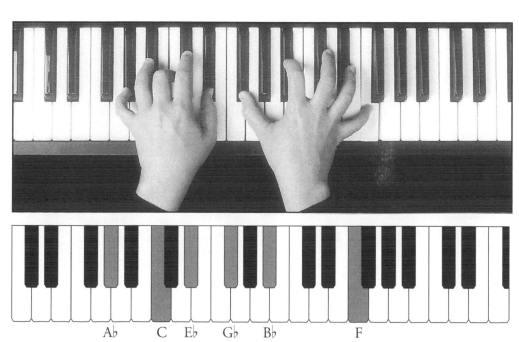

A♭   C   E♭   G♭   B♭   F

Ab major9

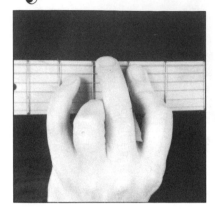
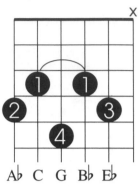

Ab C G Bb Eb

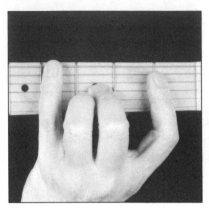
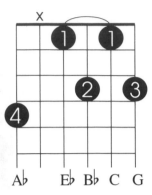

Ab Eb Bb C G

Ab major13

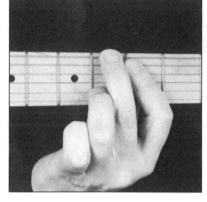
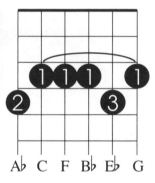

Ab C F Bb Eb G

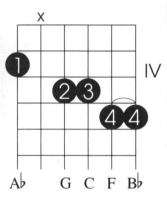

IV

Ab G C F Bb

Ab minor9

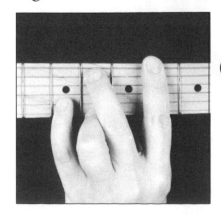
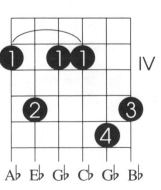

IV

Ab Eb Gb Cb Gb Bb

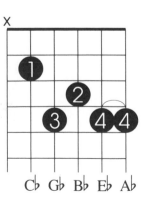

Cb Gb Bb Eb Ab

A♭ major9

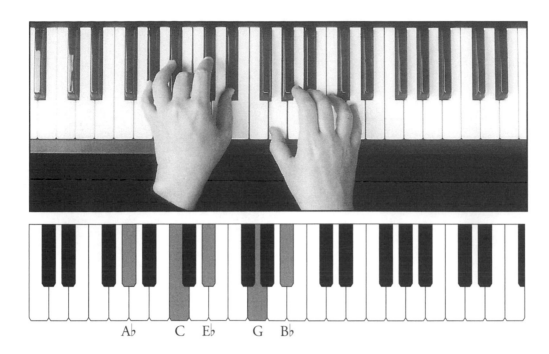

Ab   C Eb   G Bb

A♭ major13

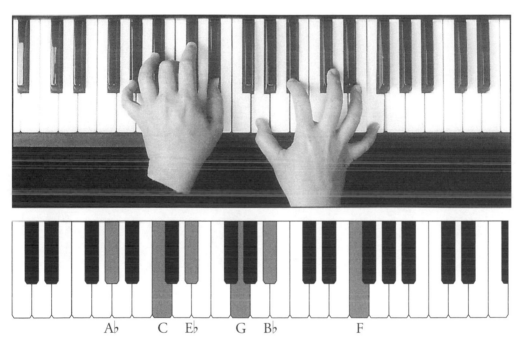

Ab   C Eb   G Bb   F

A♭ minor9

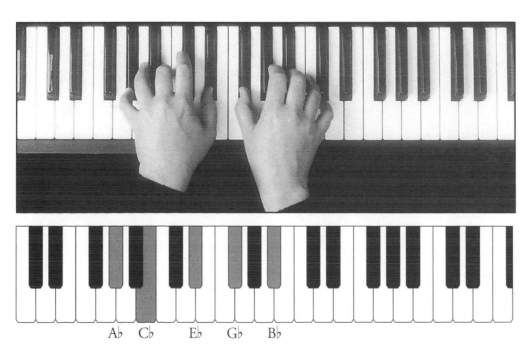

Ab Cb   Eb   Gb   Bb

Ab minor11

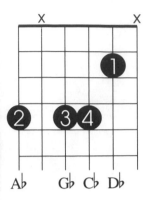

Ab Gb Cb Db

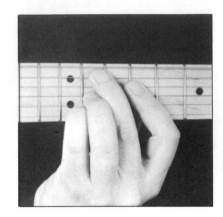
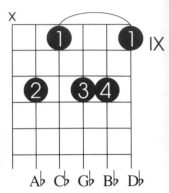

Ab Cb Gb Bb Db

Ab minor13

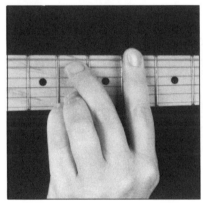
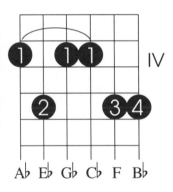

Ab Eb Gb Cb F Bb

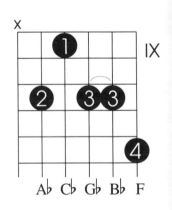

Ab Cb Gb Bb F

A♭ minor11

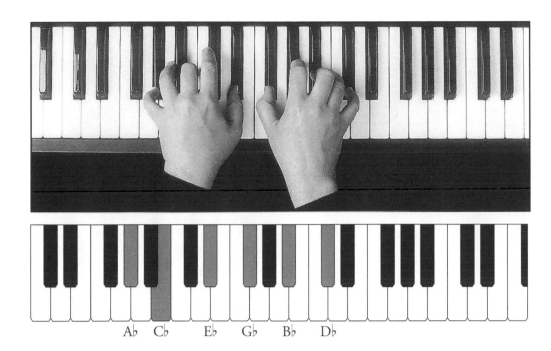

Ab   Cb   Eb   Gb   Bb   Db

A♭ minor13

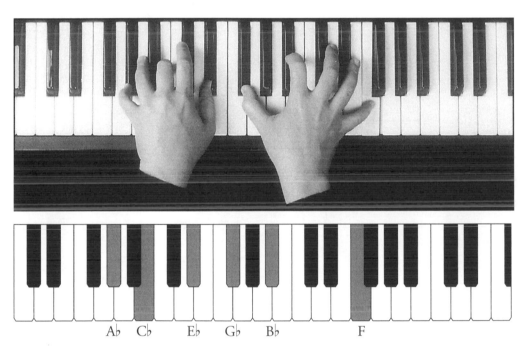

Ab   Cb   Eb   Gb   Bb   F

A Chords

A major

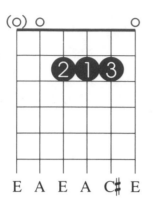

E A E A C# E

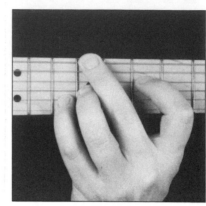

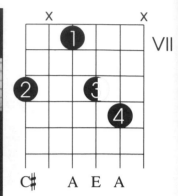

VII

C# A E A

Asus4

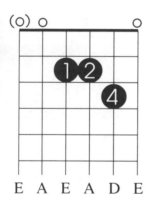

E A E A D E

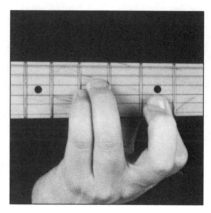

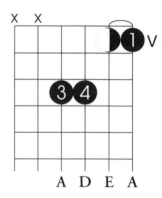

V

A D E A

A6

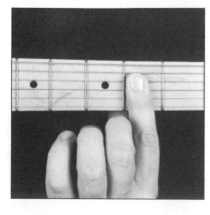

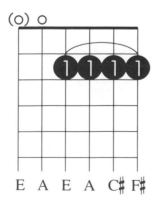

E A E A C# F#

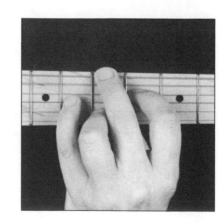

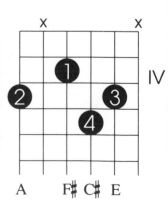

IV

A F# C# E

A major

A   C♯   E

A major *first inversion*

C♯   E   A

Asus4

A   D   E

Asus4 *first inversion*

D   E   A

A6

A   C♯   E   F♯

A6 *first inversion*

C♯   E   F♯   A

A7

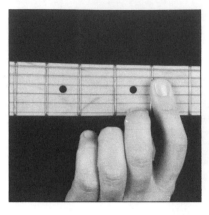

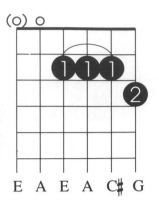

E A E A C♯ G

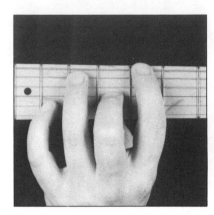

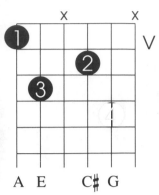

A E C♯ G

A°7

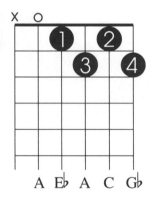

A E♭ A C G♭

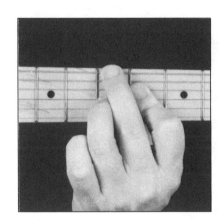

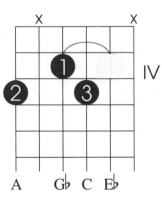

A G♭ C E♭

A major7

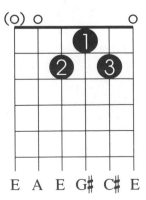

E A E G♯ C♯ E

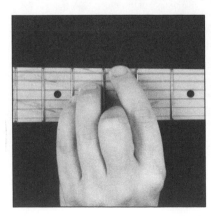

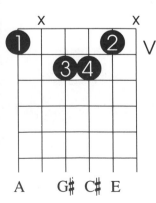

A G♯ C♯ E

A7

A C♯ E G

A7 *first inversion*

C♯ E G A

A°7

A C E♭ G♭

A°7 *first inversion*

C E♭ G♭ A

A major7

A C♯ E G♯

A major7 *first inversion*

C♯ E G♯ A

A minor

(O) o   o

E A E A C E

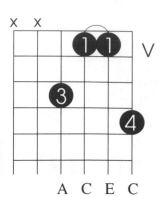

x x

V

A C E C

A minor6

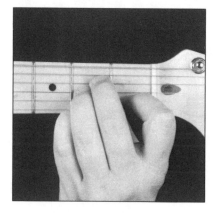

(O) o

E A E A C F#

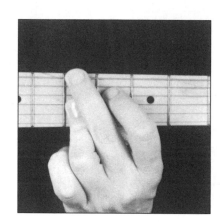

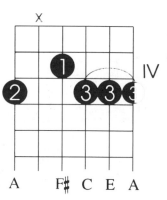

x

IV

A F# C E A

A minor7

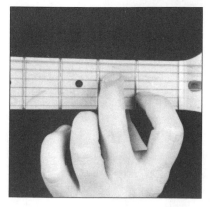

x o o o

A E G C E

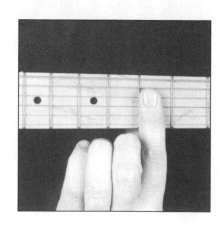

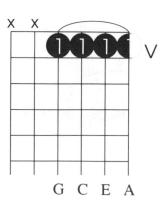

x x

V

G C E A

A minor

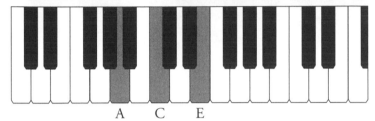

A   C   E

A minor *first inversion*

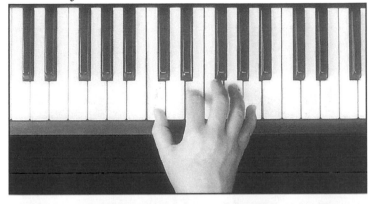

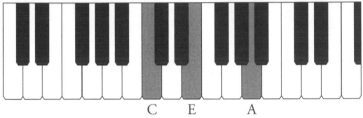

C   E   A

A minor6

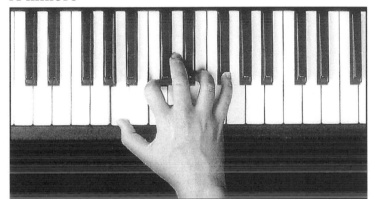

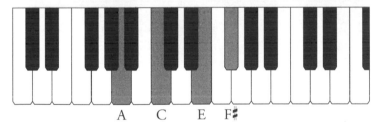

A   C   E   F♯

A minor6 *first inversion*

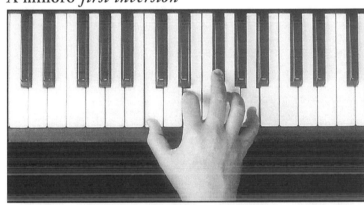

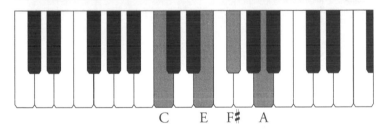

C   E F♯ A

A minor7

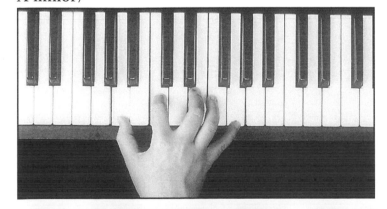

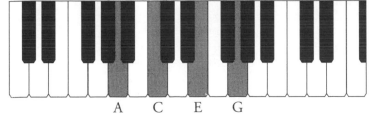

A   C   E   G

A minor7 *first inversion*

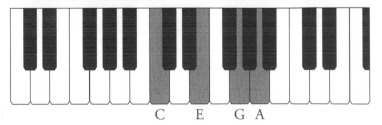

C   E   G A

A minor7♭5

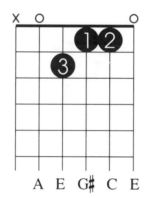

A E♭ A C G

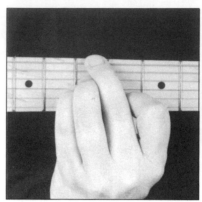

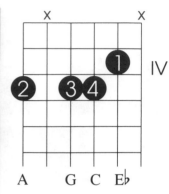

A G C E♭

IV

A minor (major7)

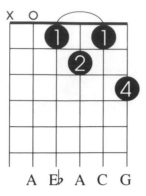

A E G♯ C E

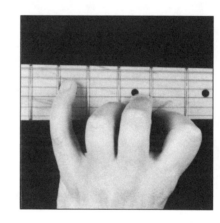

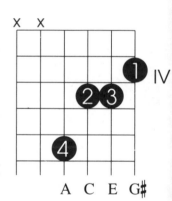

A C E G♯

IV

A minor7♭5

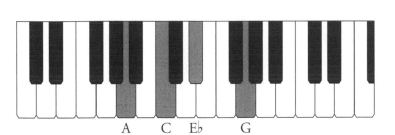

A C E♭ G

A minor7♭5 *first inversion*

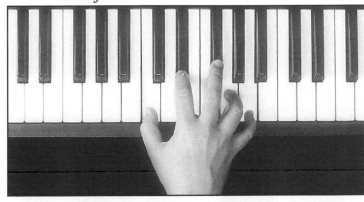

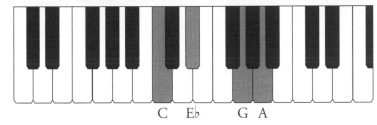

C E♭ G A

A minor (major7)

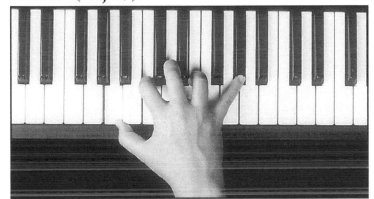

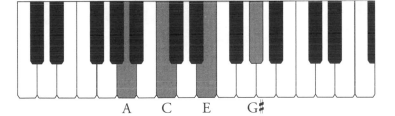

A C E G♯

A minor (major7) *first inversion*

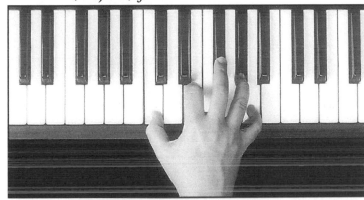

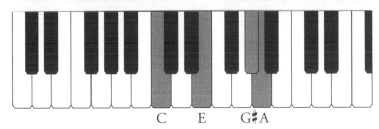

C E G♯A

A6/9

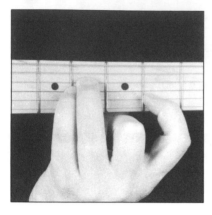

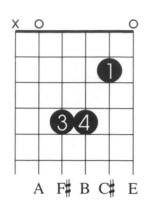

A F# B C# E

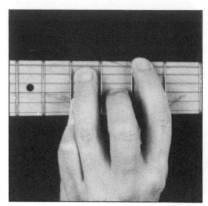

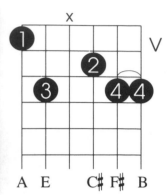

A E C# F# B

A9

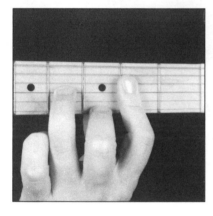

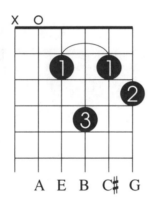

A E B C# G

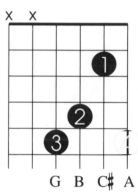

G B C# A

A9sus4

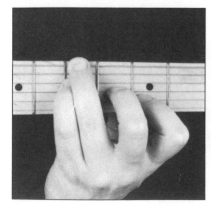

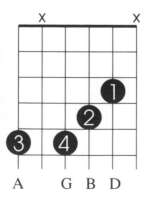

A G B D

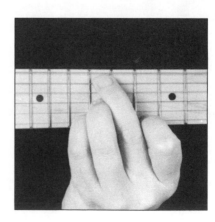

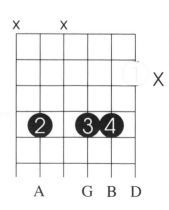

A G B D

A6/9

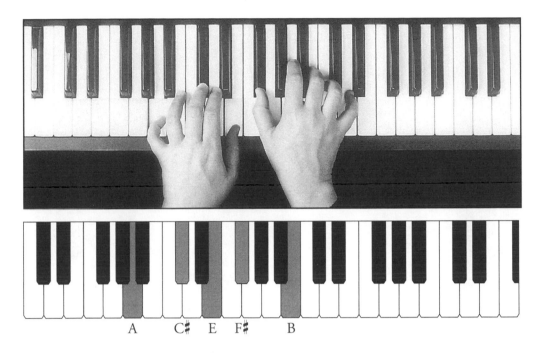

A C# E F# B

A9

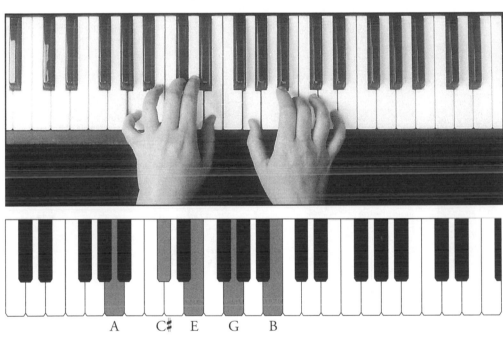

A C# E G B

A9sus4

A D E G B

A9♭5

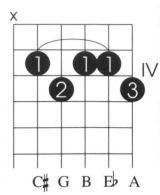

A C♯ G B E♭ — IV

C♯ G B E♭ A — IV

A9♯5

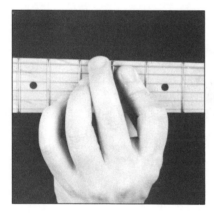

A C♯ G B E♯ — IV

A G C♯ E♯ B — V

A13

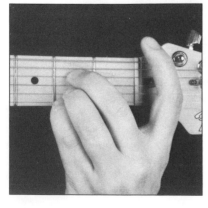

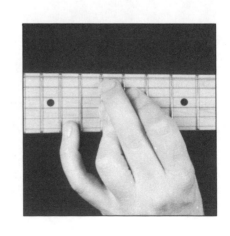

A E G C♯ F♯

A C♯ G B F♯ — XI

A9♭5

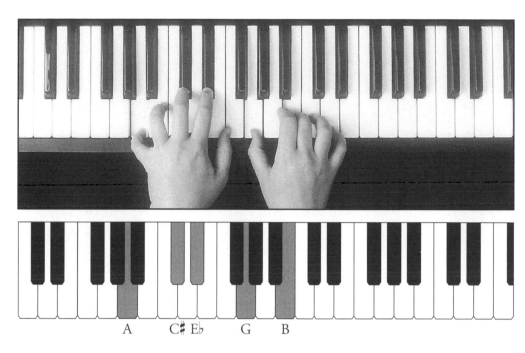

A   C♯ E♭   G   B

A9♯5

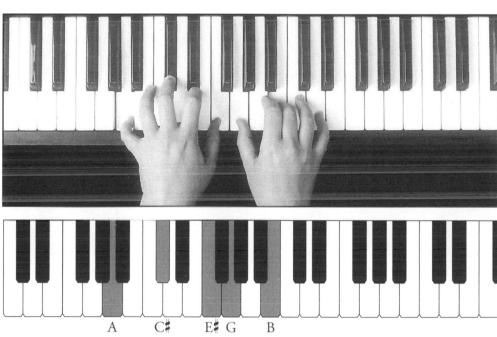

A   C♯   E♯ G   B

A13

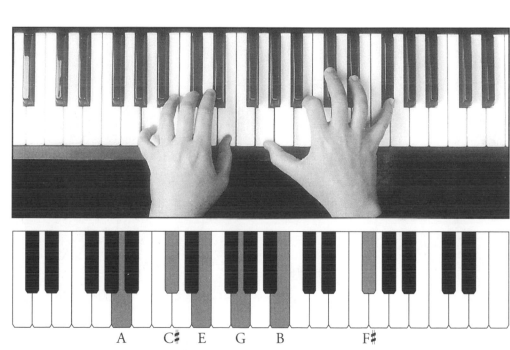

A   C♯ E   G   B   F♯

A major9

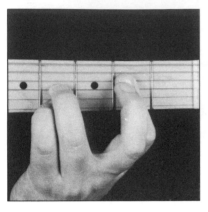
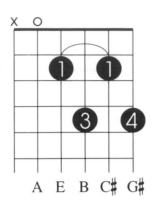

A E B C# G#

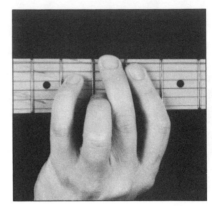
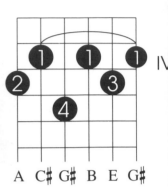

IV

A C# G# B E G#

A major13

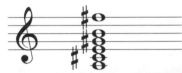

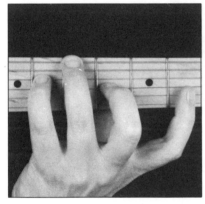
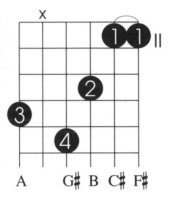

II

A G# B C# F#

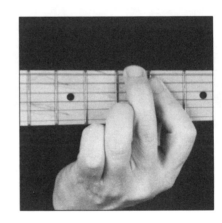
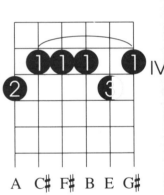

IV

A C# F# B E G#

A minor9

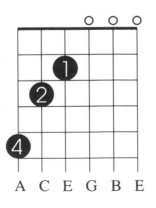

A C E G B E

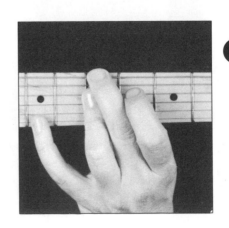
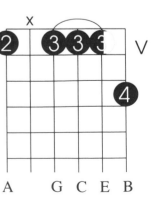

V

A G C E B

A major9

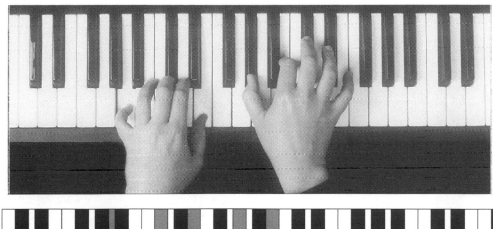

A C# E G# B

A major13

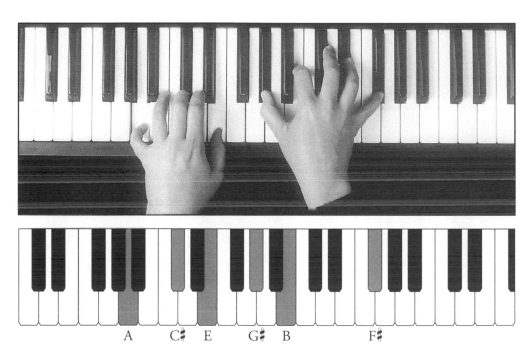

A C# E G# B F#

A minor9

A C E G B

A minor11

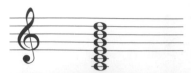

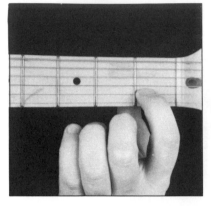

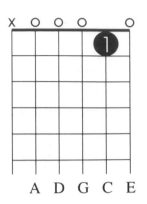

A D G C E

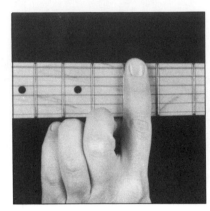

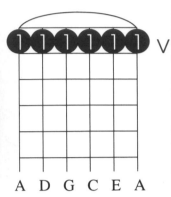

A D G C E A

A minor13

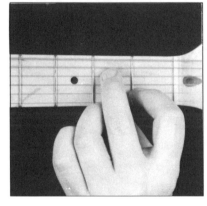

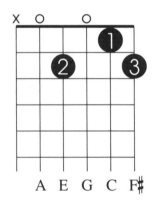

A E G C F#

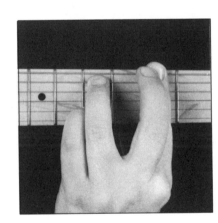

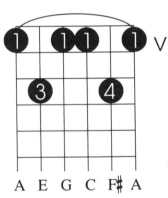

A E G C F# A

A minor11

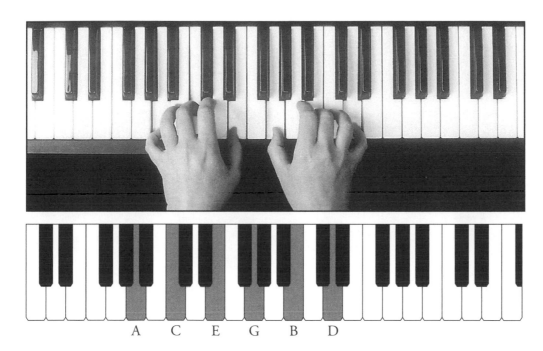

A C E G B D

A minor13

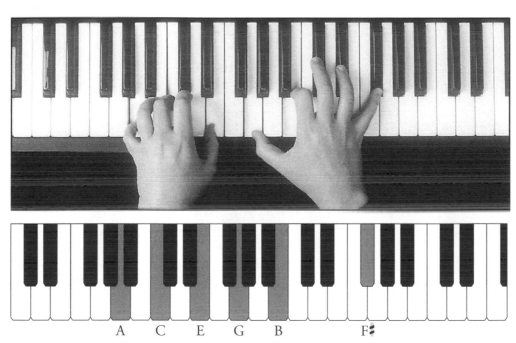

A C E G B F♯

B♭ Chords

B♭ major

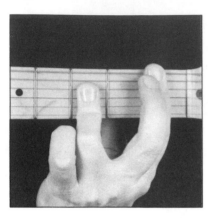

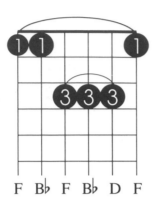

F B♭ F B♭ D F

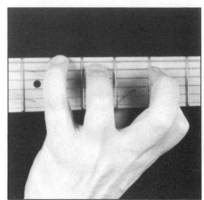

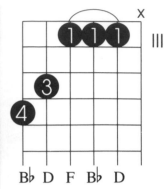

III

B♭ D F B♭ D

B♭sus4

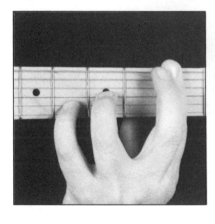

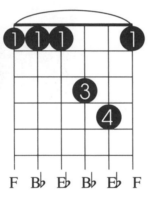

F B♭ E♭ B♭ E♭ F

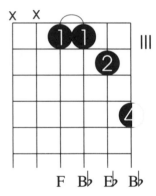

III

F B♭ E♭ B♭

B♭6

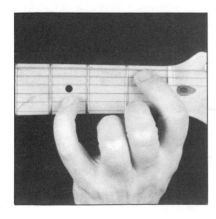

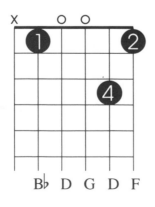

B♭ D G D F

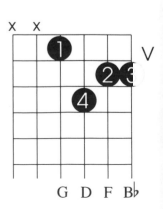

V

G D F B♭

B♭ major

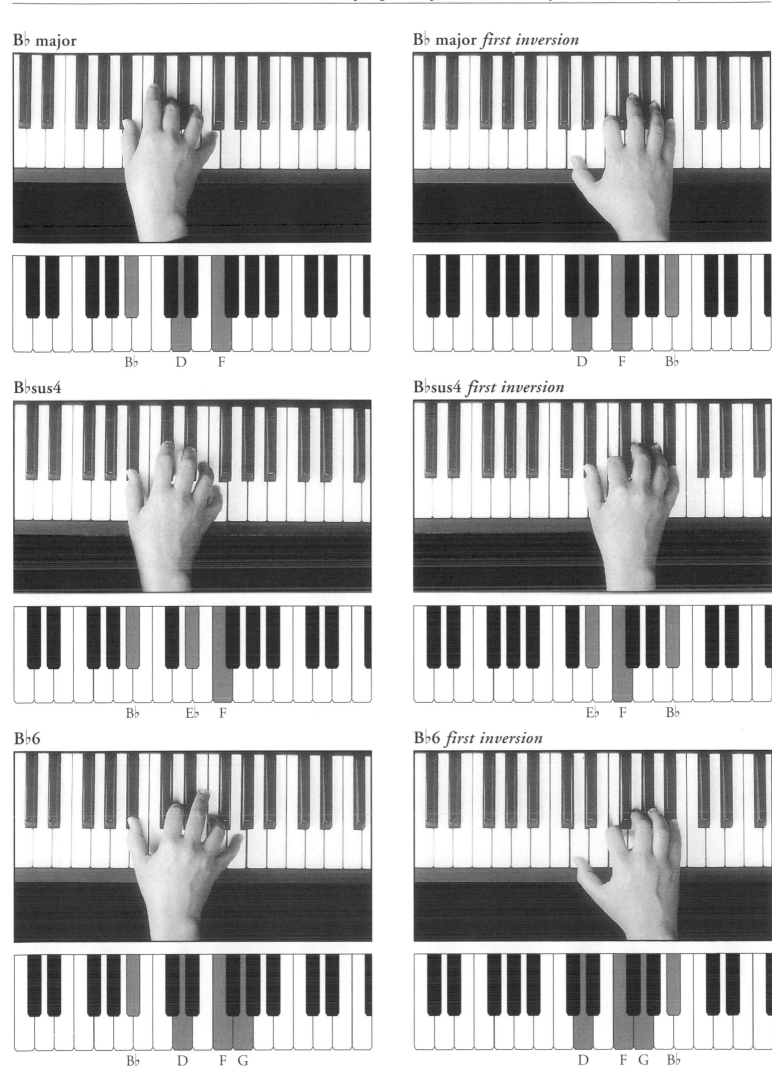

B♭　D　F

B♭ major *first inversion*

D　F　B♭

B♭sus4

B♭　E♭　F

B♭sus4 *first inversion*

E♭　F　B♭

B♭6

B♭　D　F　G

B♭6 *first inversion*

D　F　G　B♭

B♭7

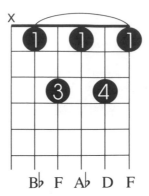

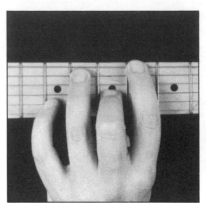

Bb F Ab D F

Bb F D Ab — VI

B♭°7

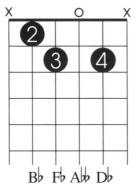

Bb Fb Abb Db

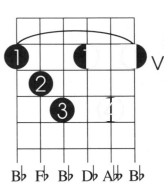

Bb Fb Bb Db Abb Bb — VI

B♭ major7

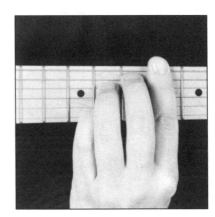

Bb F A D F

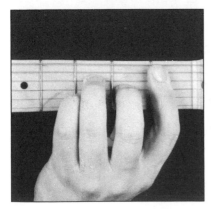

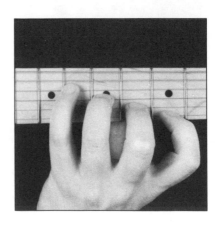

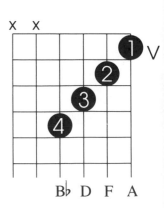

Bb D F A — V

B♭7

B♭ D F A♭

B♭7 *first inversion*

D F A♭ B♭

B♭°7

B♭ D♭ F♭ A♭♭

B♭°7 *first inversion*

D♭ F♭ A♭♭ B♭

B♭ major7

B♭ D F A

B♭ major7 *first inversion*

D F A B♭

B♭ minor

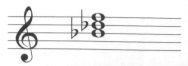

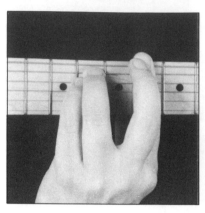
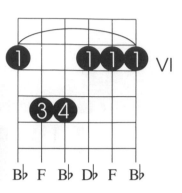

VI

Bb F Bb Db F Bb

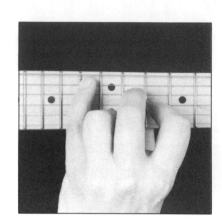
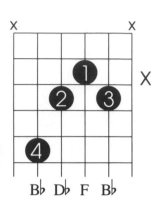

X

Bb Db F Bb

B♭ minor6

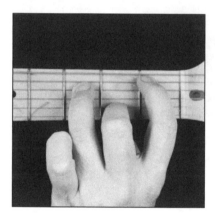
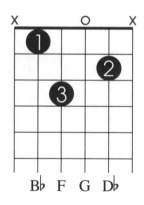

Bb F G Db

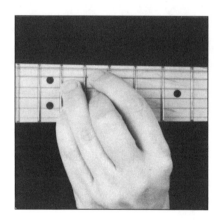
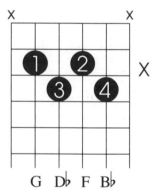

X

G Db F Bb

B♭ minor7

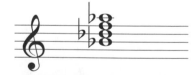

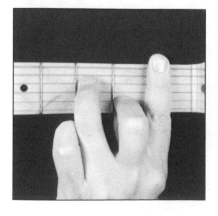
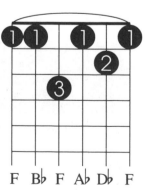

F Bb F Ab Db F

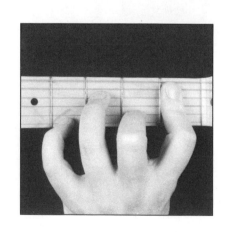
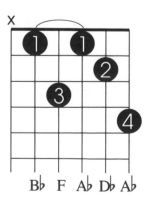

Bb F Ab Db Ab

B♭ minor

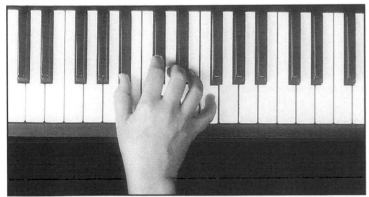

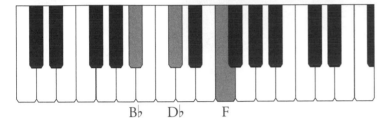

B♭ D♭ F

B♭ minor *first inversion*

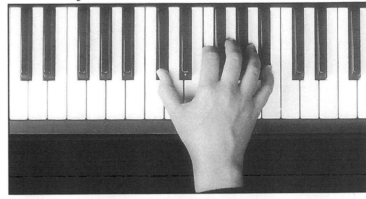

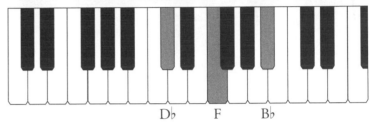

D♭ F B♭

B♭ minor6

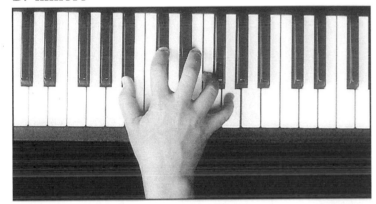

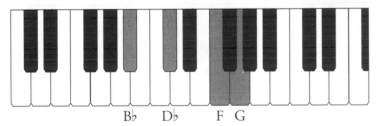

B♭ D♭ F G

B♭ minor6 *first inversion*

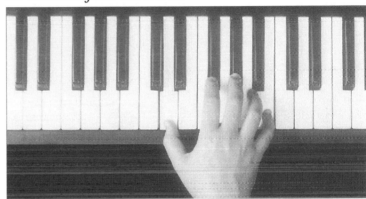

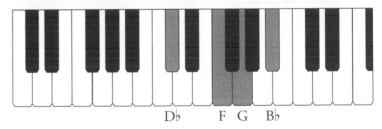

D♭ F G B♭

B♭ minor7

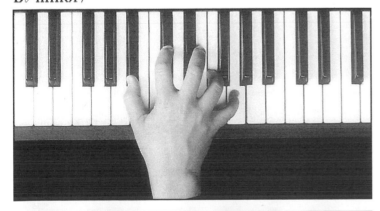

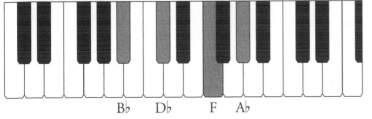

B♭ D♭ F A♭

B♭ minor7 *first inversion*

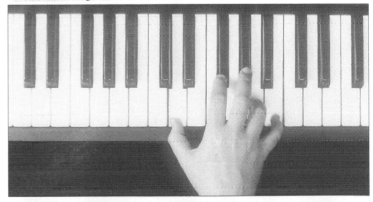

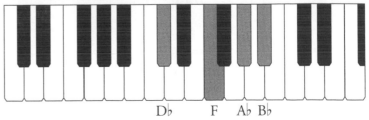

D♭ F A♭ B♭

B♭ minor7♭5

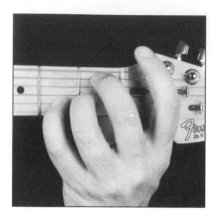 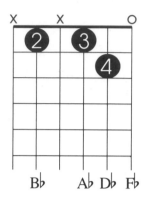

B♭ A♭ D♭ F♭

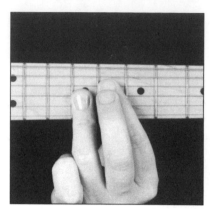 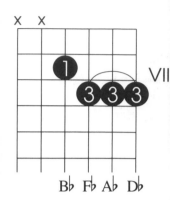

B♭ F♭ A♭ D♭

VII

B♭ minor (major7)

 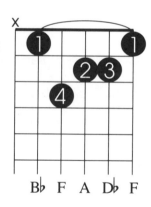

B♭ F A D♭ F

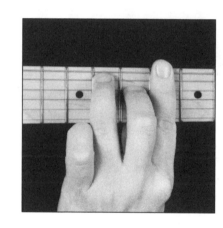 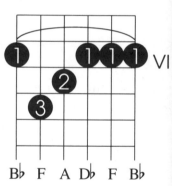

B♭ F A D♭ F B♭

VI

B♭ minor7♭5

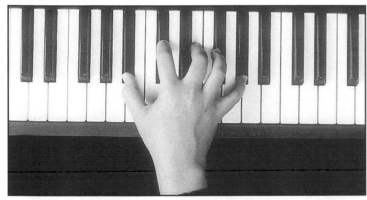

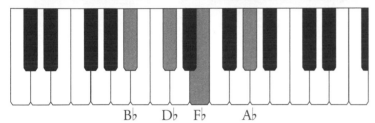

B♭   D♭   F♭   A♭

B♭ minor7♭5 *first inversion*

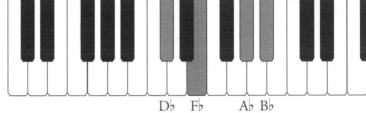

D♭   F♭   A♭ B♭

B♭ minor (major7)

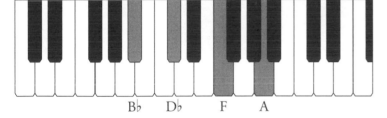

B♭   D♭   F   A

B♭ minor (major7) *first inversion*

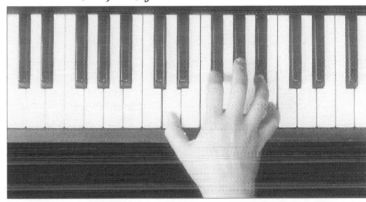

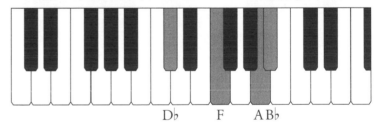

D♭   F   A B♭

B♭6/9

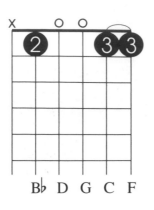

x | o | o
2 | | | 3 | 3

B♭ D G C F

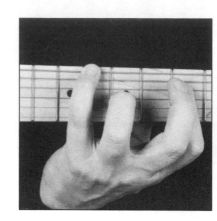

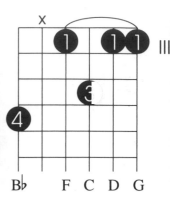

x
1 | | 1 | 1 | III
| | 3
4

B♭ F C D G

B♭9

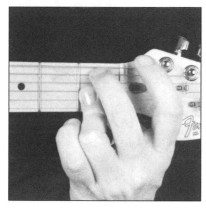

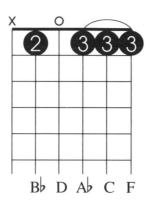

x | o
2 | | 3 | 3 | 3

B♭ D A♭ C F

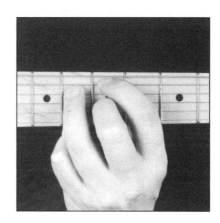

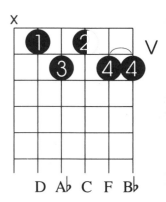

x
1 | | 2 | | V
| 3 | | 4 | 4

D A♭ C F B♭

B♭9sus4

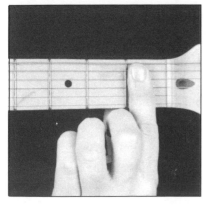

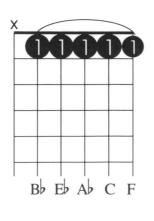

x
1 | 1 | 1 | 1 | 1

B♭ E♭ A♭ C F

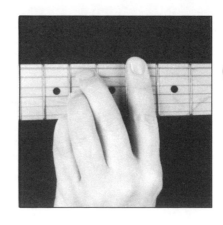

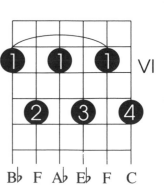

1 | | 1 | 1 | VI
| 2 | | 3 | 4

B♭ F A♭ E♭ F C

B♭6/9

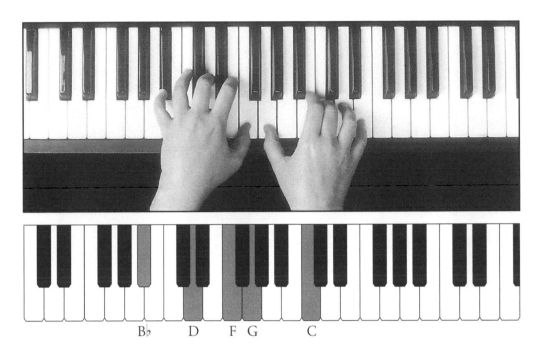

B♭ D F G C

B♭9

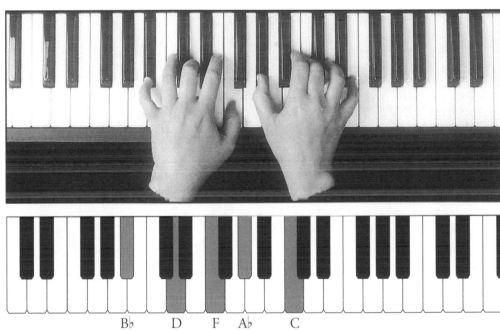

B♭ D F A♭ C

B♭9sus4

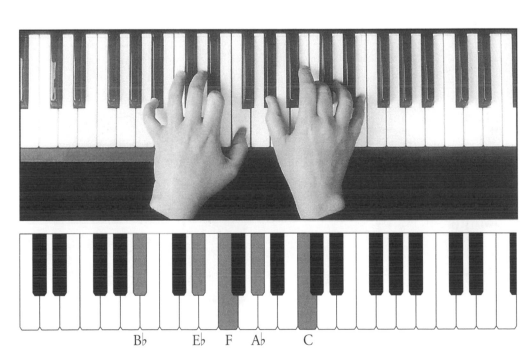

B♭ E♭ F A♭ C

Bb9b5

x   o   o

Bb D Ab C Fb

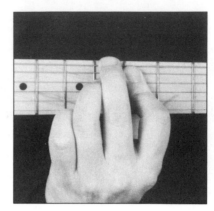

x

V

Bb D Ab C Fb

Bb9#5

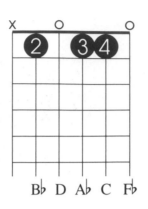

x   o

Bb D Ab C F#

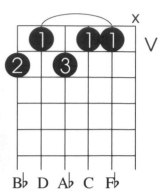

x

VI

Bb Ab D F# C

Bb13

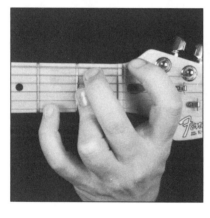

x   x

Bb Ab D G

x

VI

Bb Ab D G C

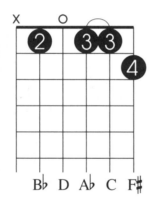

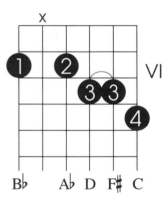

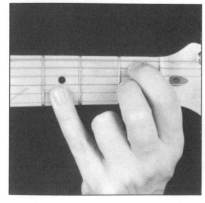

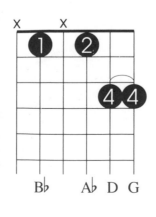

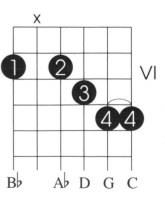

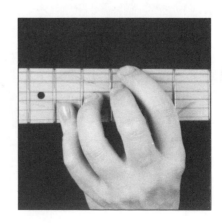

B♭9♭5

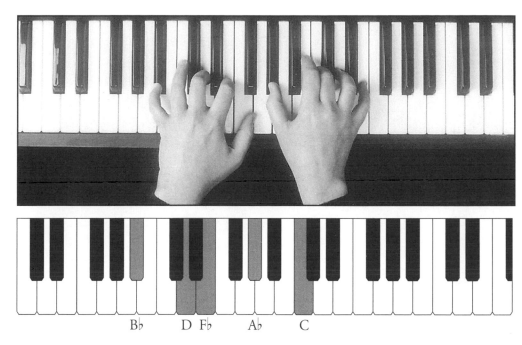

B♭ D F♭ A♭ C

B♭9♯5

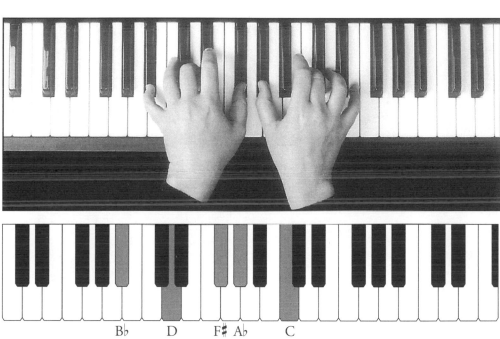

B♭ D F♯ A♭ C

B♭13

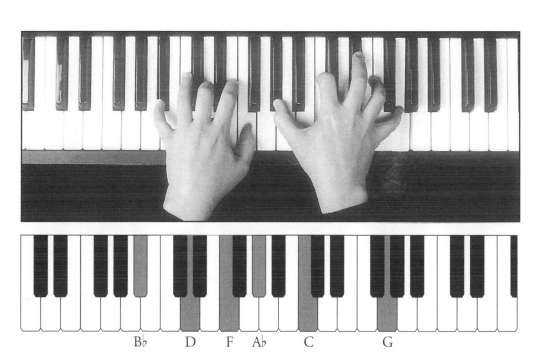

B♭ D F A♭ C G

B♭ major9

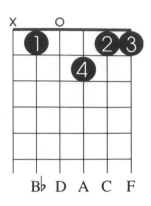

B♭ D A C F

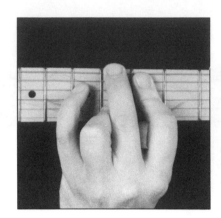

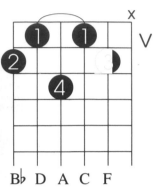

B♭ D A C F

B♭ major13

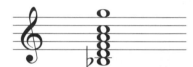

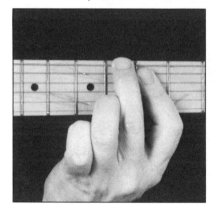

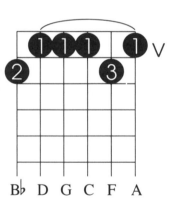

B♭ D G C F A

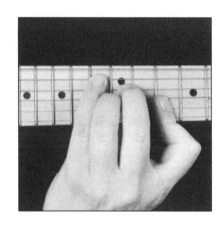

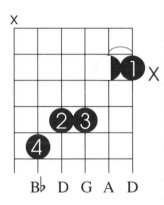

B♭ D G A D

B♭ minor9

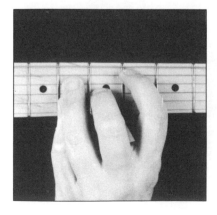

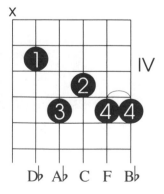

D♭ A♭ C F B♭

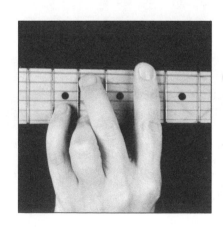

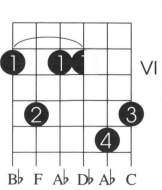

B♭ F A♭ D♭ A♭ C

B♭ major9

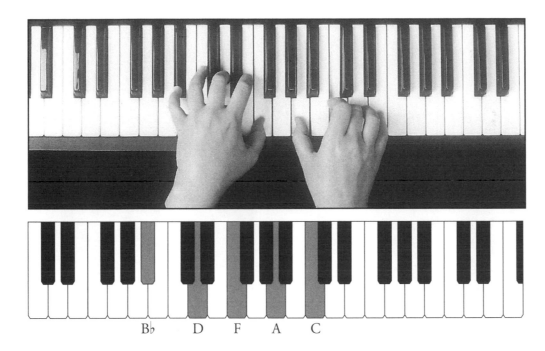

B♭   D   F   A   C

B♭ major13

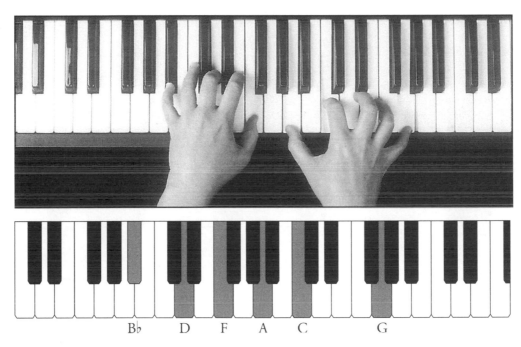

B♭   D   F   A   C   G

B♭ minor9

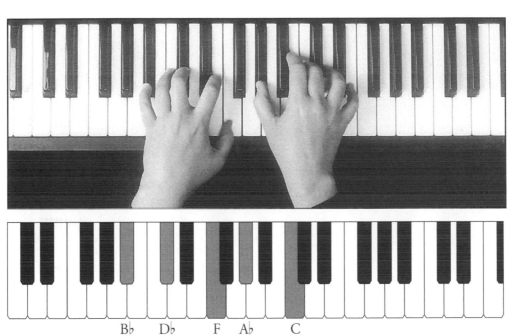

B♭   D♭   F   A♭   C

Bb minor11

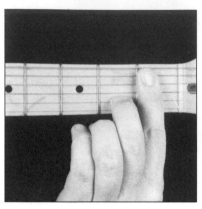

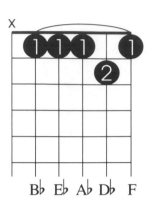

Bb Eb Ab Db F

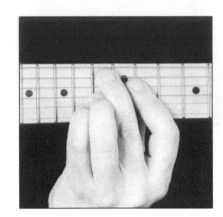

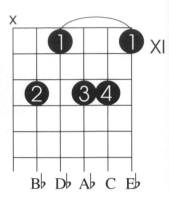

XI

Bb Db Ab C Eb

Bb minor13

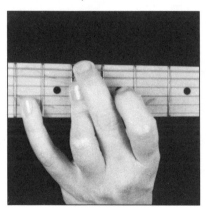

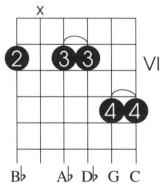

VI

Bb Ab Db G C

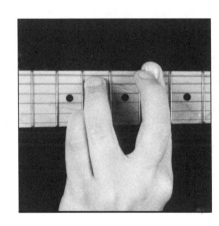

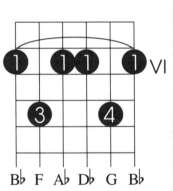

VI

Bb F Ab Db G Bb

B♭ minor11

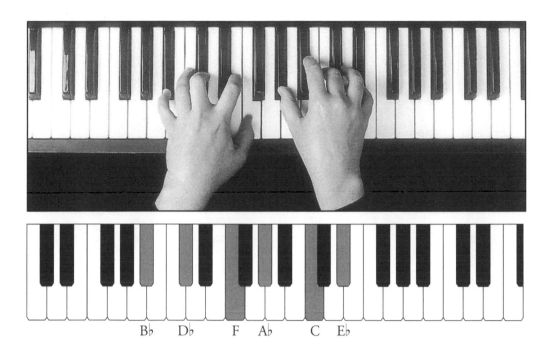

B♭ D♭ F A♭ C E♭

B♭ minor13

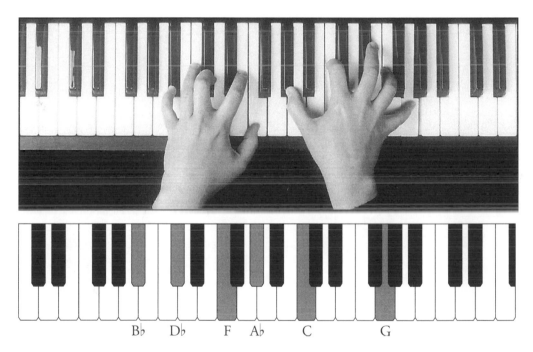

B♭ D♭ F A♭ C G

B Chords

B major

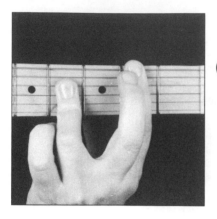 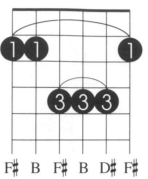

F# B F# B D# F#

 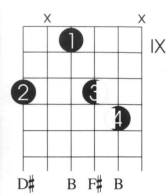

IX

D# B F# B

Bsus4

 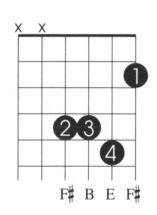

F# B E F#

 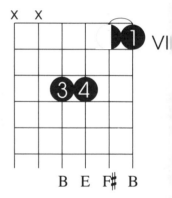

VI

B E F# B

B6

 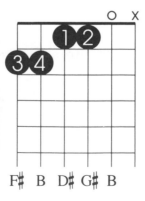

F# B D# G# B

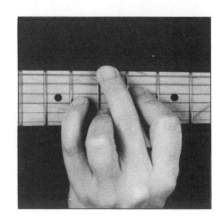 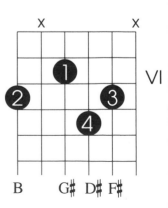

VI

B G# D# F#

B major

B   D#   F#

B major *first inversion*

D#   F#   B

Bsus4

B   E   F#

Bsus4 *first inversion*

E   F#   B

B6

B   D#   F# G#

B6 *first inversion*

D#   F# G#   B

B7

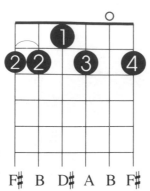

F♯ B D♯ A B F♯

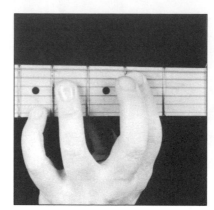
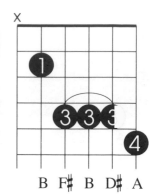

B F♯ B D♯ A

B°7

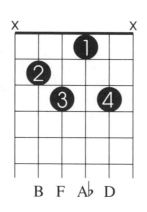

B F A♭ D

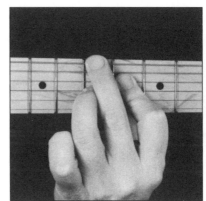
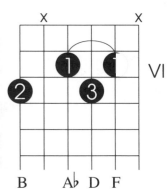

B A♭ D F

VI

B major7

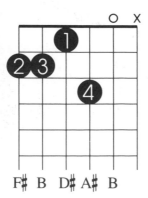

F♯ B D♯ A♯ B

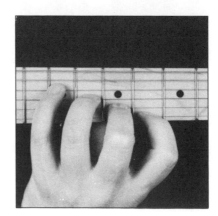
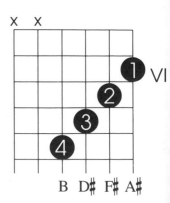

B D♯ F♯ A♯

VI

B7

B7 *first inversion*

B°7

B°7 *first inversion*

B major7

B major7 *first inversion*

B minor

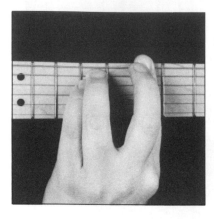
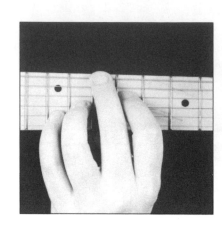

B F# B D F# B   VII

D   B F# B   IX

B minor6

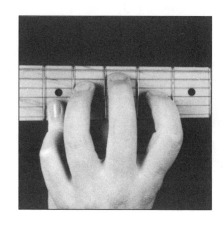

B   G# D F#

D G# B F# B   IV

B minor7

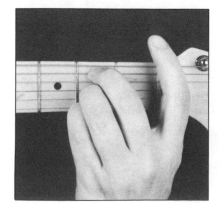
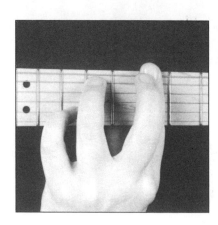

B D A B F#

B F# A D A B   VII

B minor

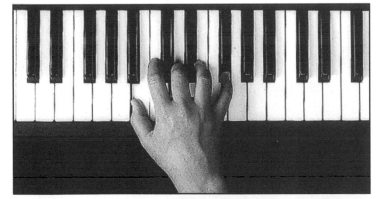

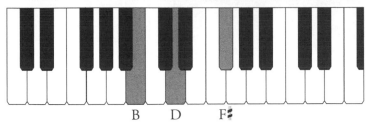

B   D   F♯

B minor *first inversion*

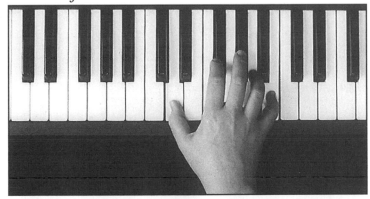

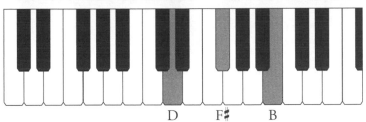

D   F♯   B

B minor6

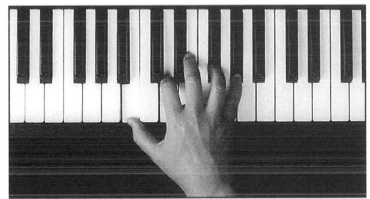

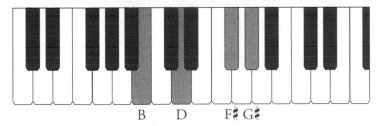

B   D   F♯ G♯

B minor6 *first inversion*

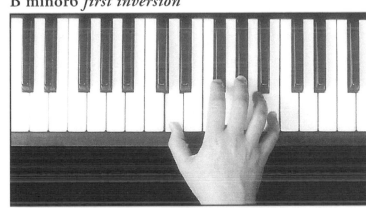

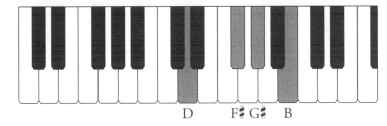

D   F♯ G♯   B

B minor7

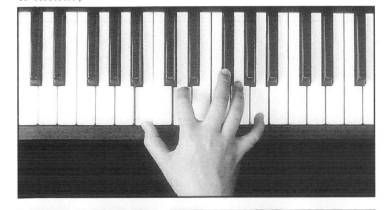

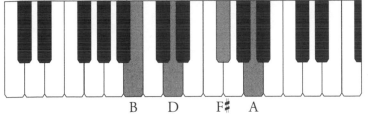

B   D   F♯   A

B minor7 *first inversion*

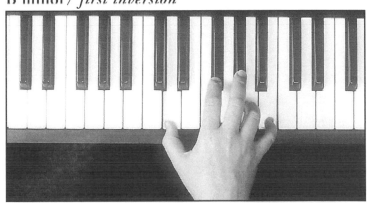

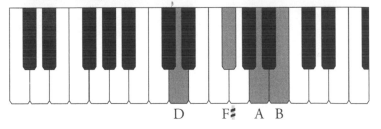

D   F♯   A B

B minor7♭5

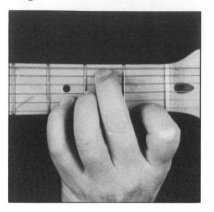
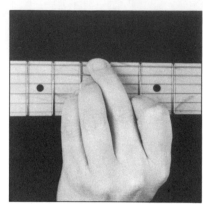
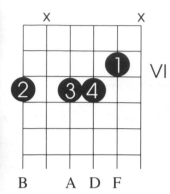

B   A D F

B   A D F

VI

B minor (major7)

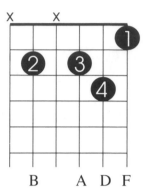
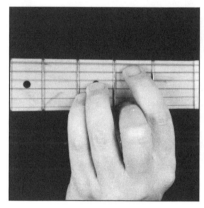
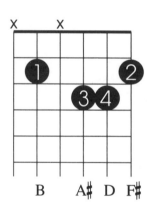
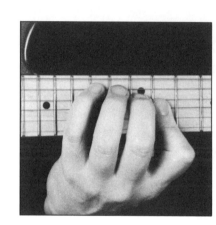
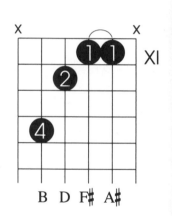

B   A♯ D F♯

B D F♯ A♯

XI

B minor7♭5

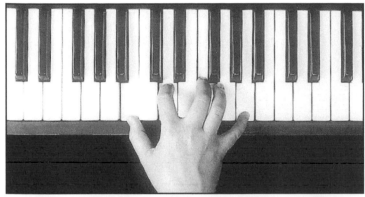

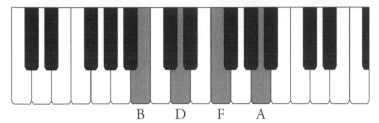

B D F A

B minor7♭5 *first inversion*

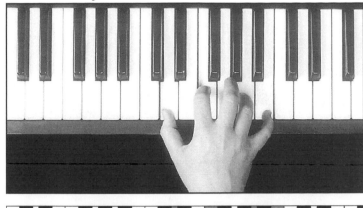

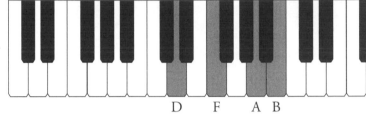

D F A B

B minor (major7)

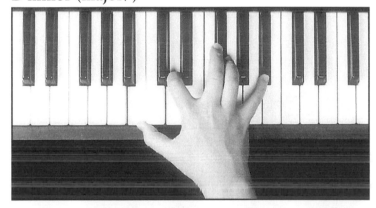

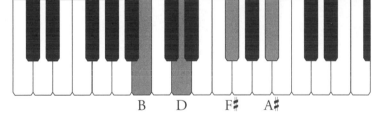

B D F♯ A♯

B minor (major7) *first inversion*

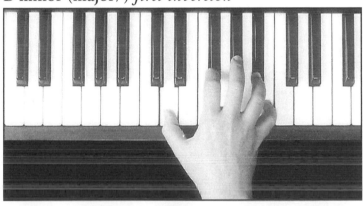

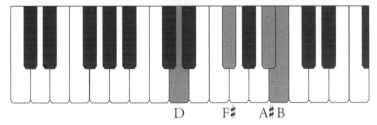

D F♯ A♯ B

B6/9

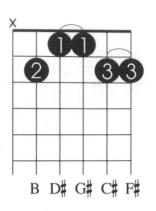

B D# G# C# F#

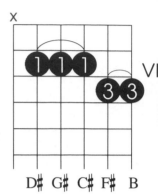

D# G# C# F# B

VI

B9

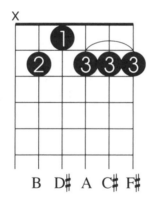

B D# A C# F#

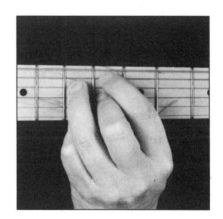

D# A C# F# B

VI

B9sus4

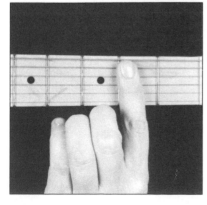

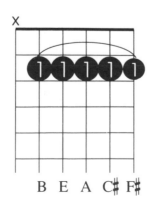

B E A C# F#

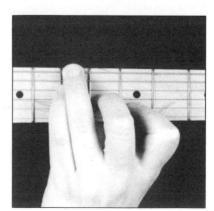

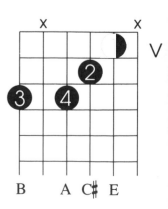

B A C# E

V

B6/9

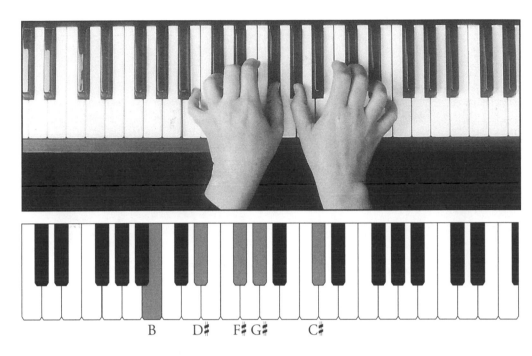

B   D♯   F♯ G♯   C♯

B9

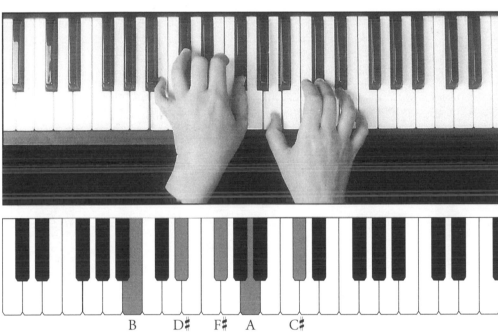

B   D♯   F♯   A   C♯

B9sus4

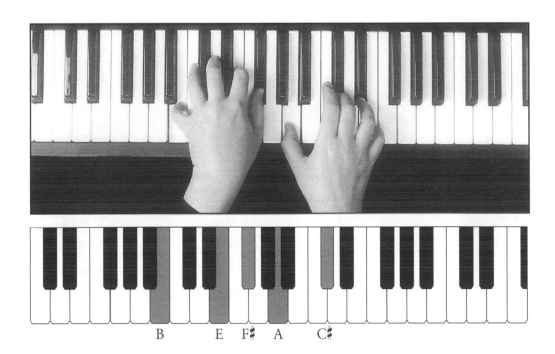

B   E F♯   A   C♯

B9♭5

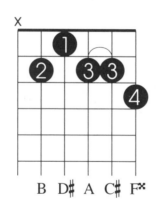

B D♯ A C♯ F

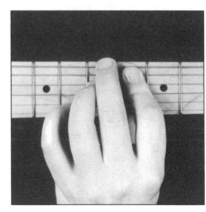

B D♯ A C♯ F

VI

B9♯5

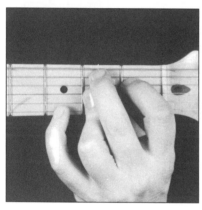

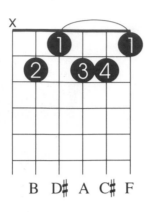

B D♯ A C♯ F𝄪

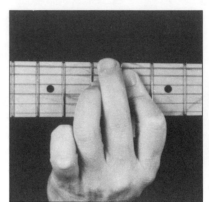

B D♯ A C♯ F𝄪

VI

B13

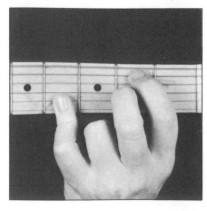

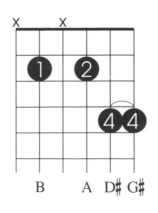

B   A D♯ G♯

B F♯ A D♯ G♯ C♯

VII

B9♭5

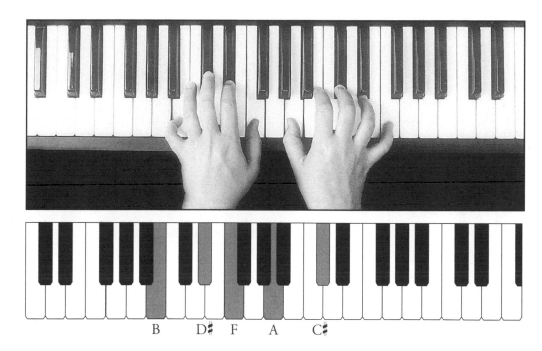

B   D♯   F   A   C♯

B9♯5

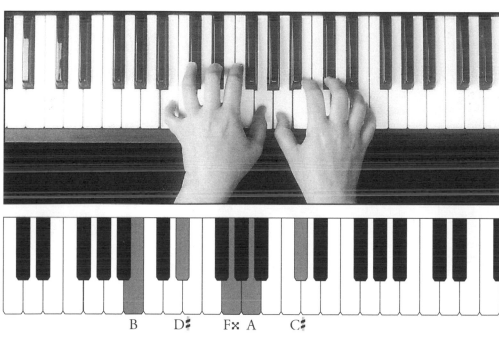

B   D♯   F✗ A   C♯

B13

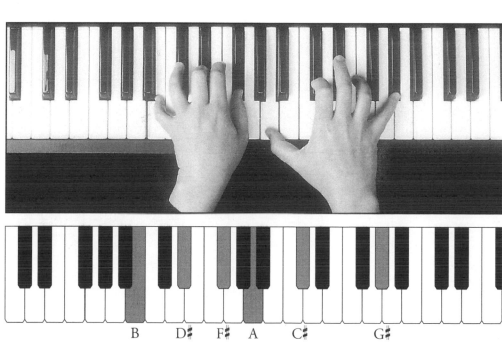

B   D♯   F♯   A   C♯   G♯

B major9

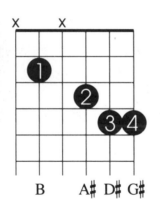

B D# A# C# F#

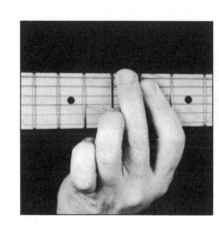

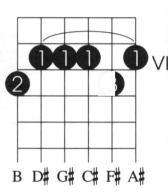

B D# A# C# F# A#

B major13

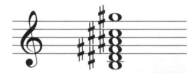

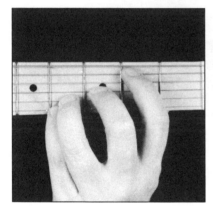

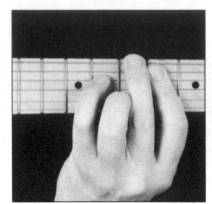

B A# D# G#

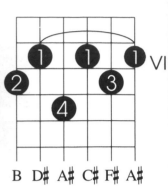

B D# G# C# F# A#

B minor9

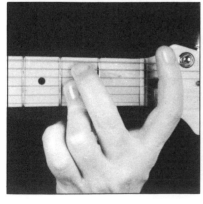

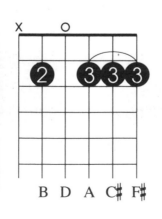

B D A C# F#

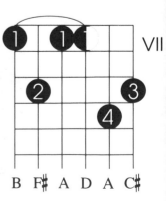

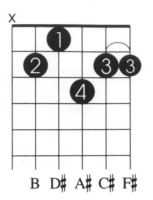

B F# A D A C#

B major9

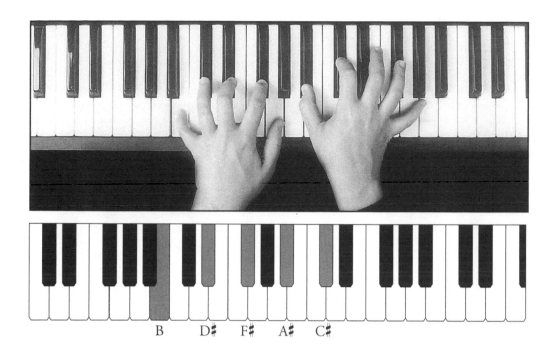

B   D#   F#   A#   C#

B major13

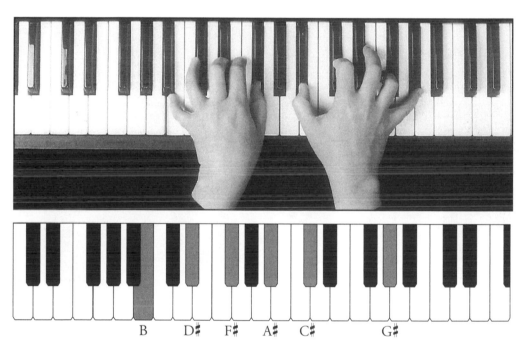

B   D#   F#   A#   C#   G#

B minor9

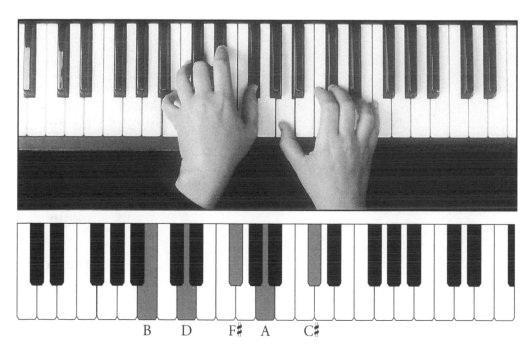

B   D   F#   A   C#

B minor11

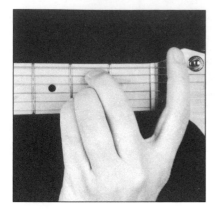

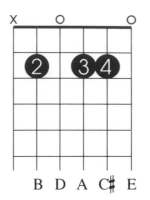

B D A C# E

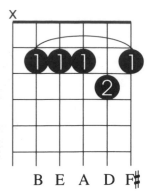

B E A D F#

B minor13

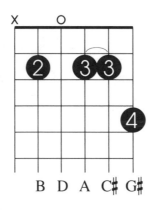

B D A C# G#

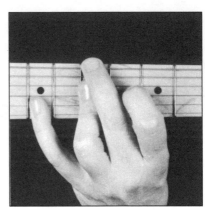

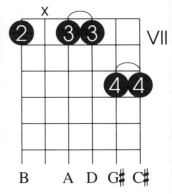

VII

B A D G# C#

B minor11

B   D   F♯   A   C♯   E

B minor13

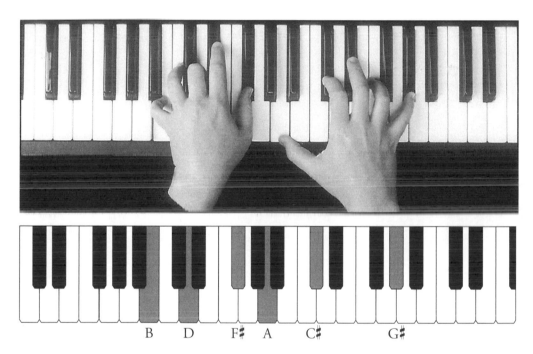

B   D   F♯   A   C♯   G♯

Progressions

The chord progression of a piece of music is its harmonic framework. As you become familiar with the different types of music you will find various forms of progressions. One of the most popular and widely used is the I-IV-V, which was derived from early blues styles. Simply stated I, IV, and V are the first, fourth, and fifth steps of a scale. The following examples are in the key of E, so the chords that would correspond to this progression are E major, A major, and B major.

This example shows the chords of the I-IV-V progression in the root position. (see page 10)

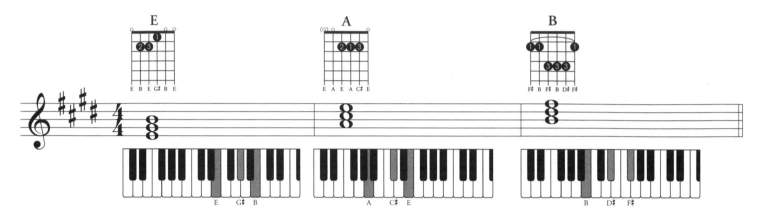

Now try using different inversions in this progression. Instead of playing the whole progression in the root position use the second inversion (see page 10) for the A and B chords. You will find it is much easier to play these inversions instead of moving your hands up and down the keyboard in the root position. Also, notice that different inversions will make whatever you're playing more harmonically interesting.

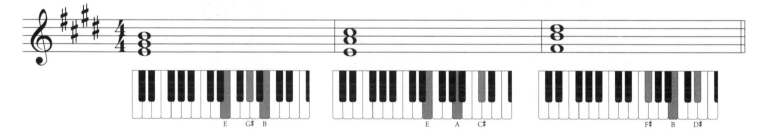

Try playing this twelve-bar progression using the chord inversions of the previous example. If you have a tape recorder or some type of sequencer, use it to record the keyboard part and then play different forms of the E, A, and B guitar chords along with the progression. Listen how the harmonic structure changes by using different chords with different voicings.

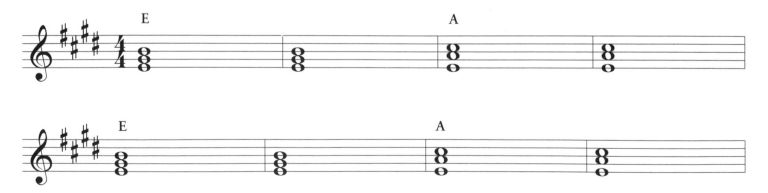

Try recording the keyboard part of this progression in the root position, along will the different forms of the guitar chords and listen to what happens harmonically.

Let's make the keyboard part a little fuller by adding a bass line. The simplest way to accomplish this is to play the root of the chord as a single whole note throughout a whole measure.

Play this twelve-bar progression using the added bass line.

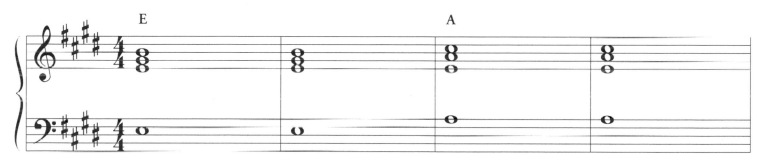

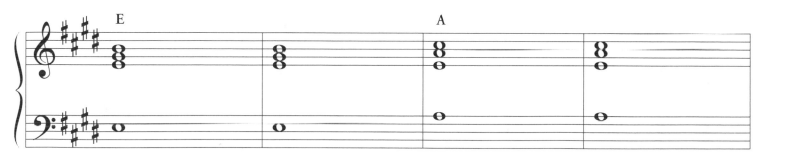

Let's make our keyboard part a little more interesting by *arpeggiating* the chords. An *arpeggio* is playing the tones of a chord in even succession. This is sometimes referred to as a *broken chord*.

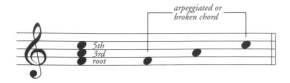

This example shows E, A, and B chords and the notes that make-up their arpeggiations.

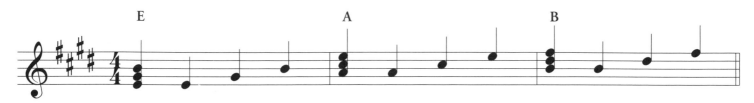

Play this twelve-bar progression with the E, A, and B chords argeggiated. Make sure you play the notes fluid and even. To create a different feel try using the sustain pedal, or consider playing the progression with the arpeggiation staccatoed.

Play the progression again with this bass line. This is similiar to the bass line on the previous page, but there's an added note an octave lower.

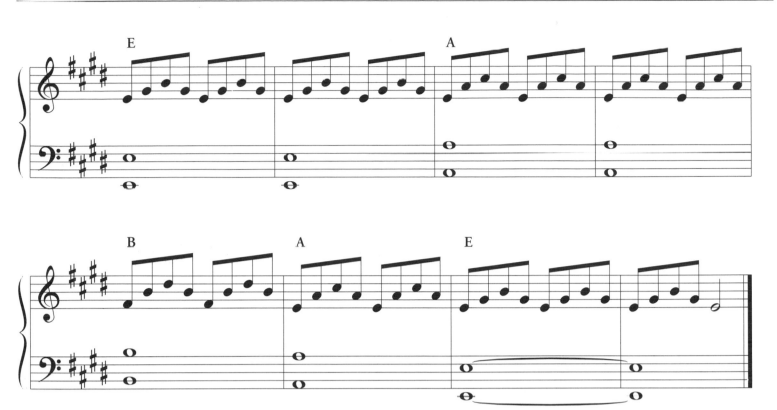

This time play the argeggiation with the left hand and the chords with the right.

Let's spice things up a bit. Using the same twelve-bar progression we are going to add a dominant seven to the E, A, and B chords.

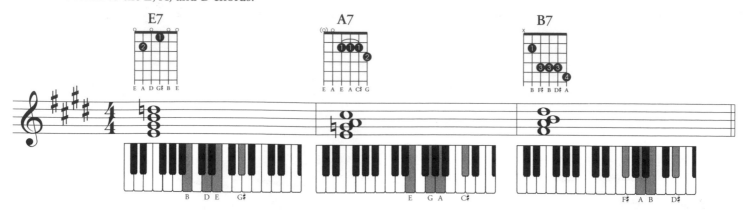

Now play the I-IV-V progression with the arpeggiated dominant seven chords. Notice that the arpeggiation is played with eighth-note triplets instead of straight eighths.

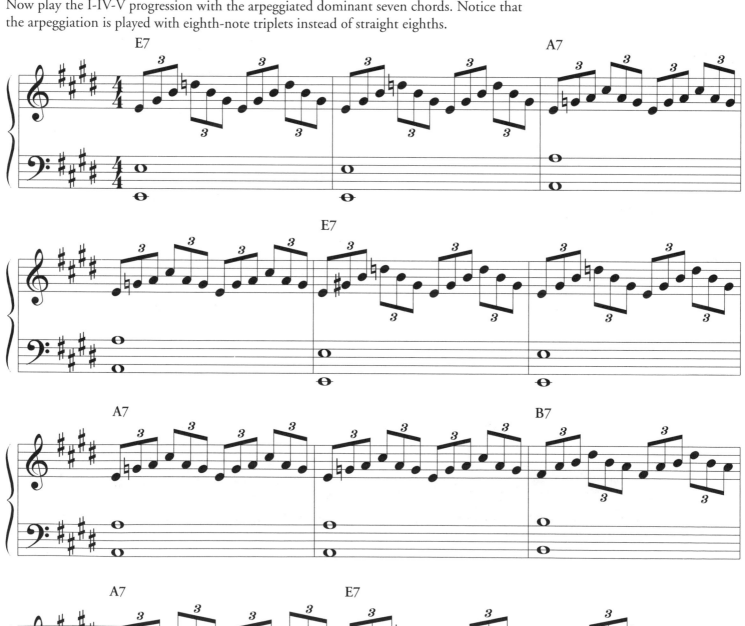

Up till now the guitar part has just consisted of block chords. Now, using the movable chords forms found on pages 217 and 218, play the guitar part in unison with the arpeggiated right hand of the keyboard part. Also, try playing the right hand of the keyboard part using block chords and let the guitar play the arpeggiated solo.

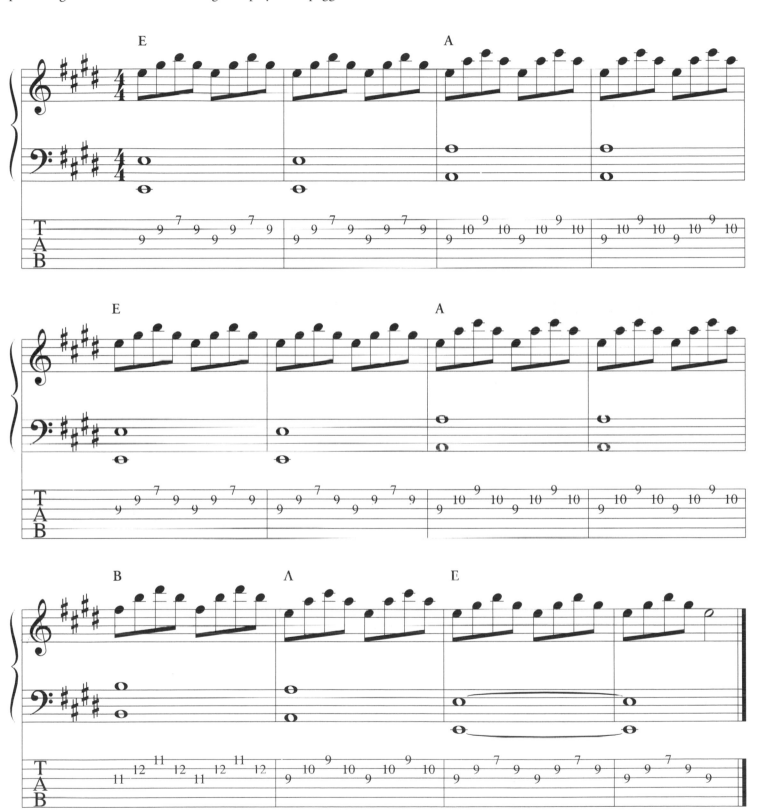

Let's add some rhythm to the keyboard part. The right hand is using the same chord inversions as in previous examples, except this time play the eighth-, quarter-note rock pattern as shown below. The left hand, instead of playing whole notes, is playing a quarter note pattern. Experiment with the guitar part, try playing with the arpeggiation pattern of the previous example or just use long sustaining chords.

Now that you have played a rock rhythm you might want to try other rhythms. The following is a list of rhythms in different styles.

Funk

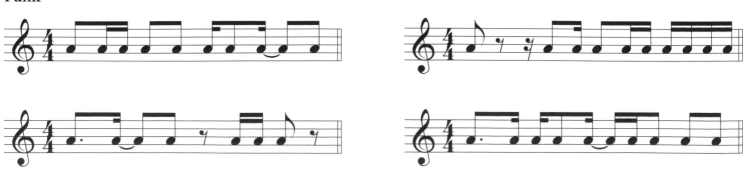

Jazz and Blues

Swing

Latin

Rock

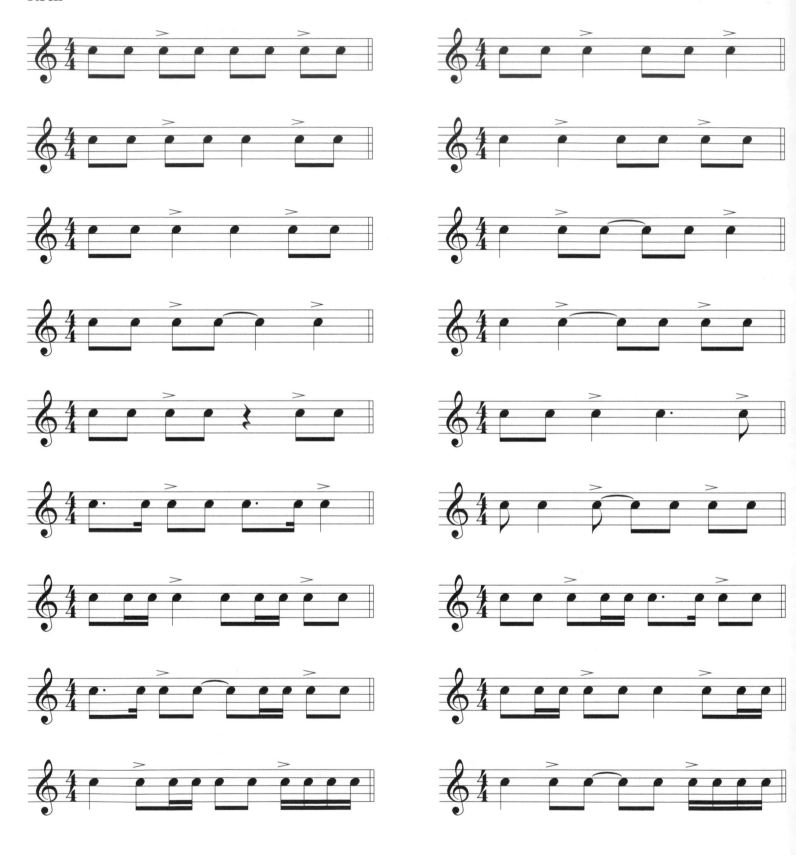

Shuffle

Moveable Chords

The moveable chords on the following pages are very helpful to the learning process of any guitarist. A knowledge of these chords allows you to move up and down the neck smoothly. As you use more complex chords—such as sevenths, ninths, thirteenths, etc.—you will have more possibilities for inversions. These inversions are indispensable when you are accompanying yourself or others; they add more depth and color to your overall arrangement. These forms are also useful for lead playing—by taking the chords in any progression and moving them up and down the neck, you will find many combinations of notes to use in your solos and fills.

The diagrams in this section are the same as the ones on previous pages with the following exceptions: First, you will notice the introduction of a black square with a finger number inside. This indicates the root of the chord, also the way the chord will be named. Below is a diagram of a guitar neck with all the note names from the nut to the twelfth fret. By learning the notes on the fingerboard you will find it easier to use all of the chords in this book and to understand their relationships to one another. To name a chord, just find the root name in the guitar-neck diagram. Then combine the root name with chord type above the chord diagram. For example, the first chord on page 217 is a major form and the root (in the diagram) is F#; therefore, the chord is F# major. If you were to move this form up one fret, the chord would become G major. The other exception is a gray square, which indicates the root when the root is not part of the chord.

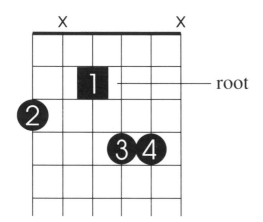
root

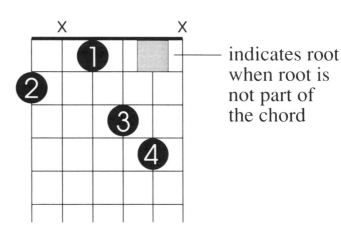
indicates root when root is not part of the chord

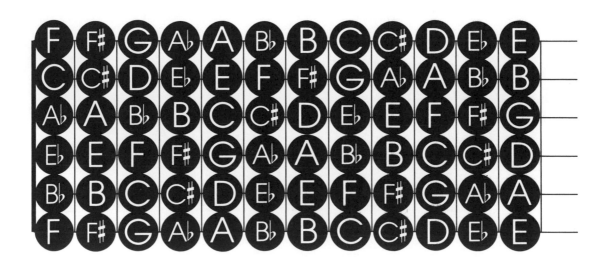

216

major

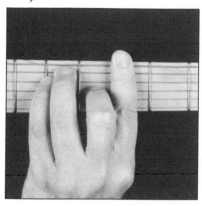
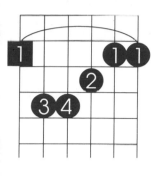

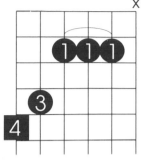

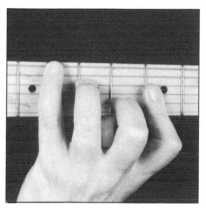
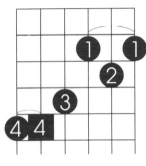

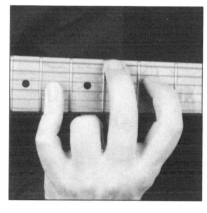
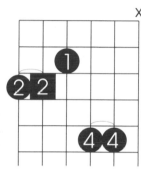

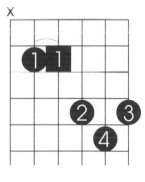

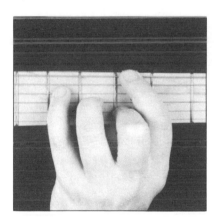
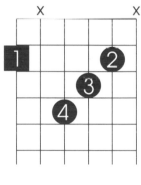

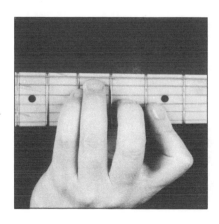

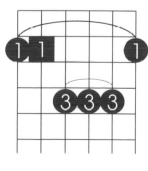
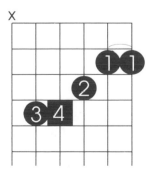

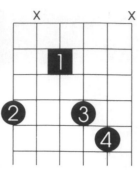

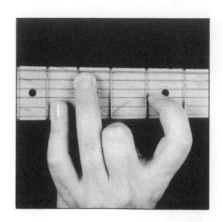
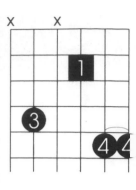

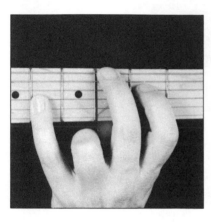
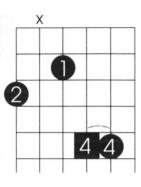

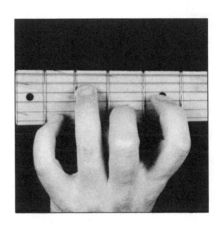
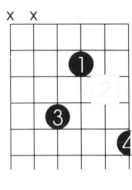

sus4

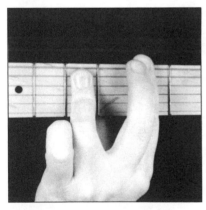
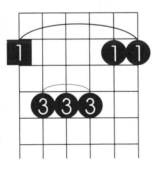

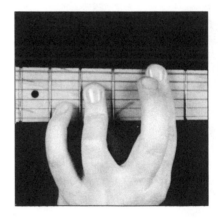
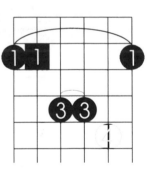

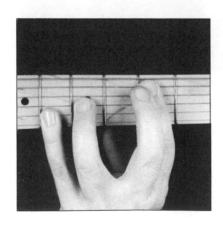
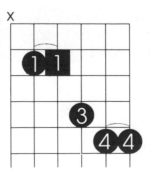

6

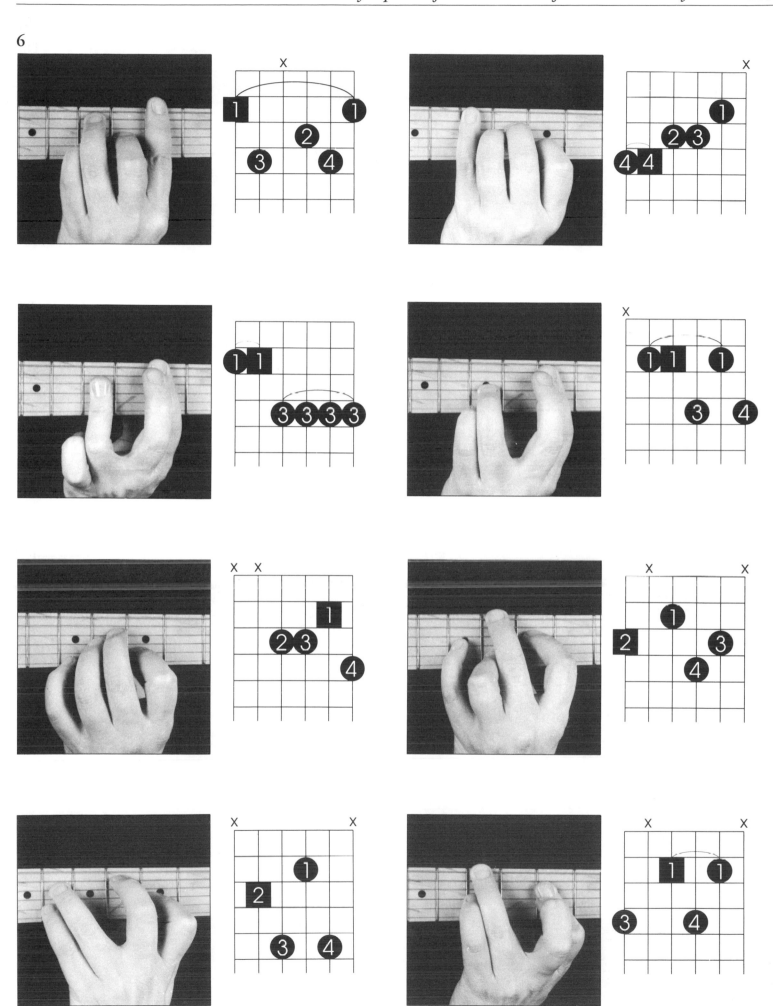

7

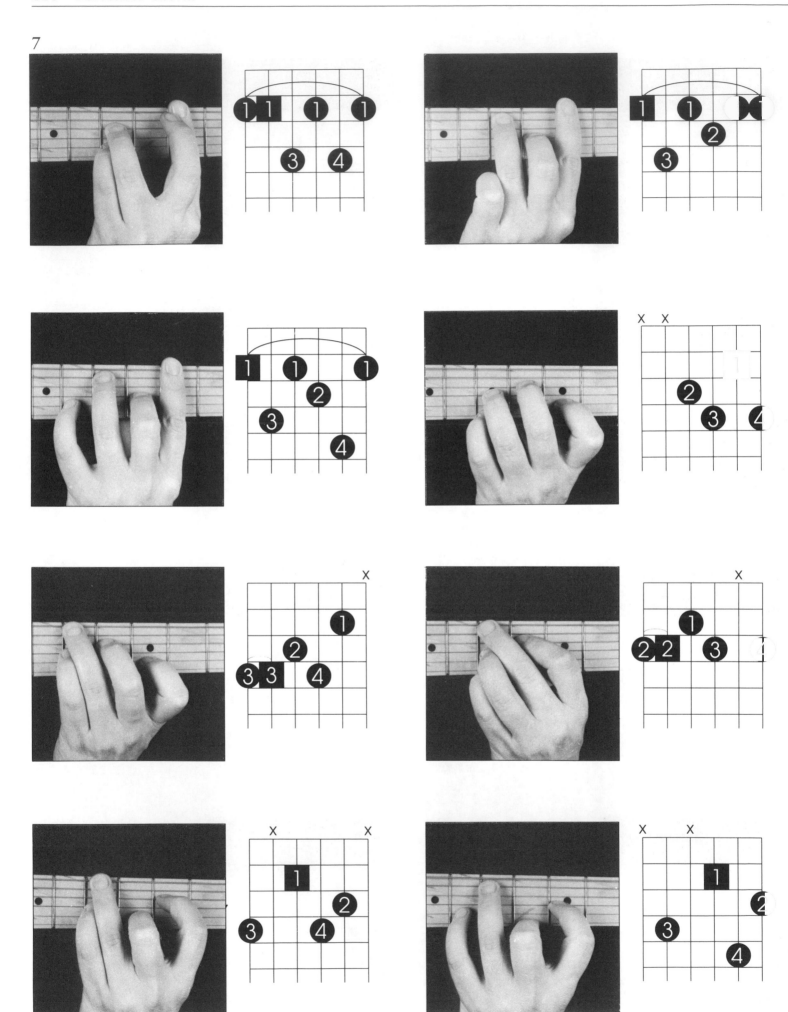

°7*

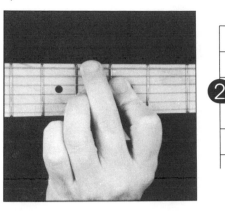
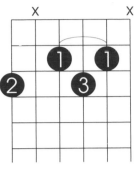

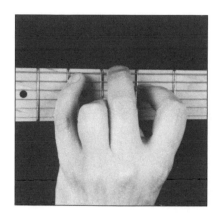
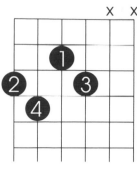

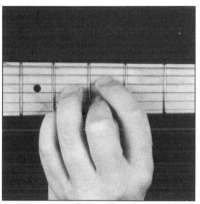
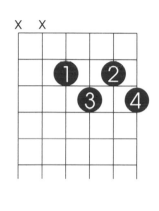

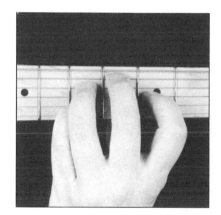
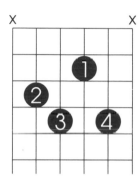

* Any note of the chord may be the root of the °7

major7

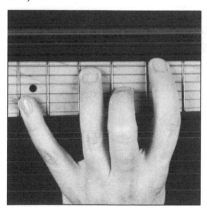
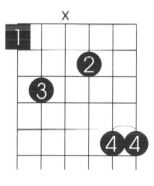

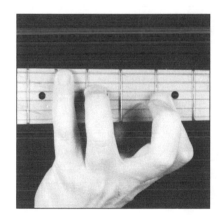
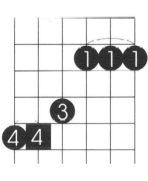

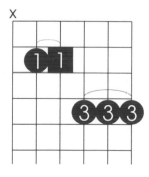

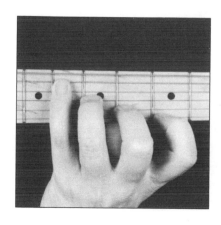
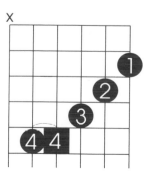

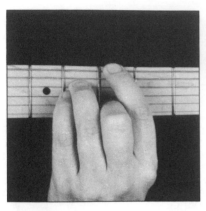
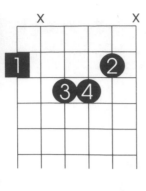

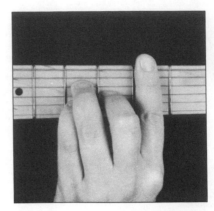
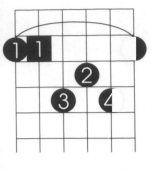

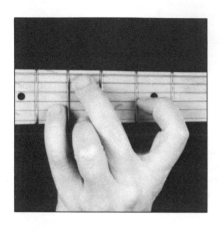
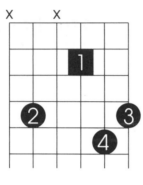

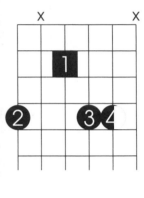

minor

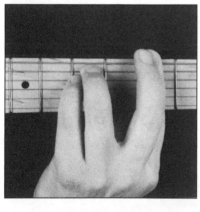
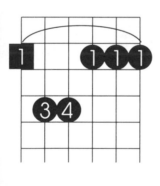

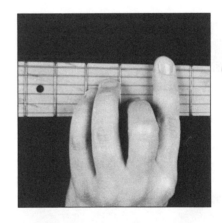
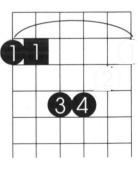

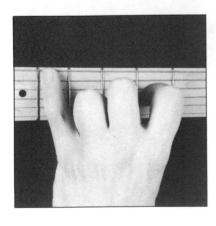
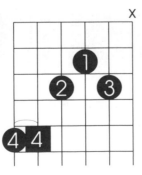

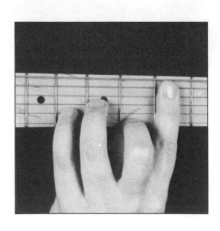
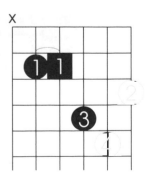

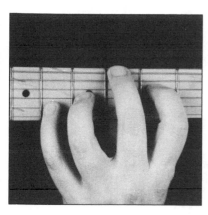
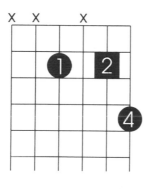

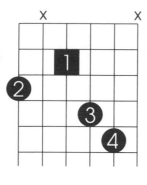
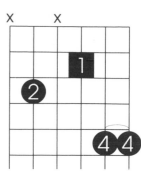

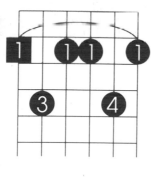

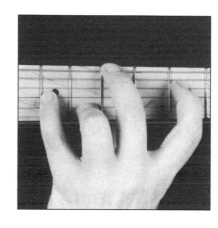
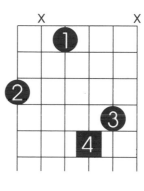

minor6

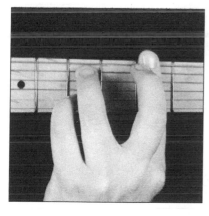
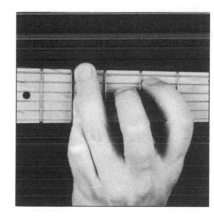

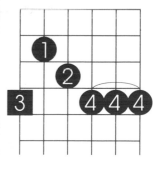
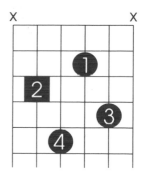

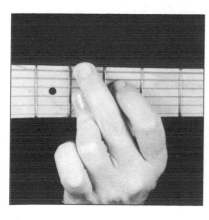
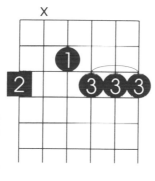

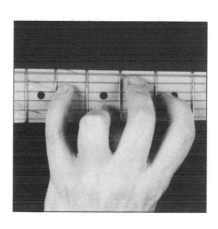
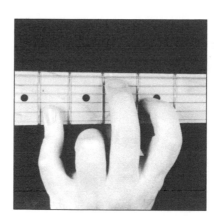

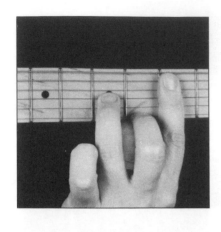
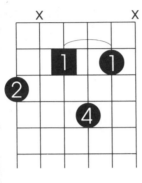

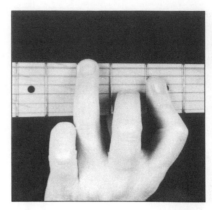
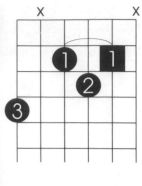

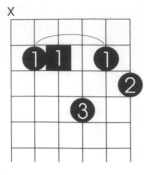

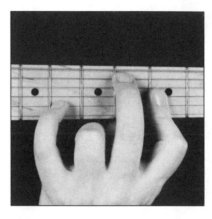
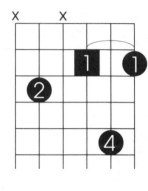

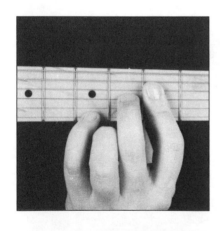
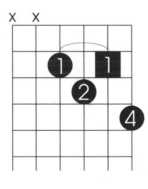

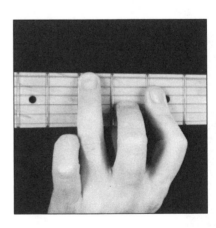
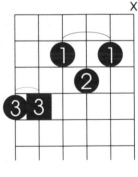

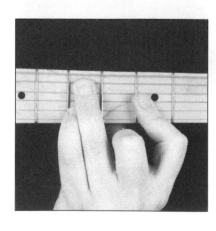
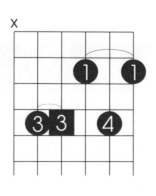

minor7

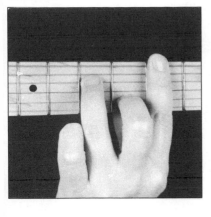
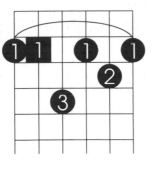

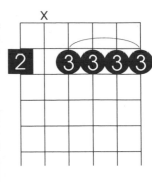

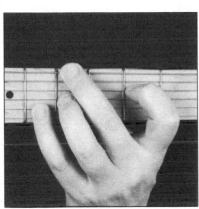
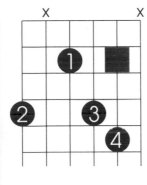
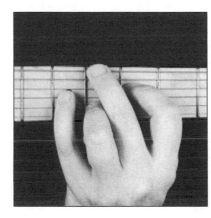
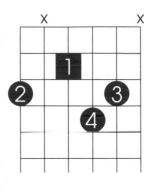

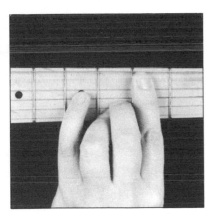
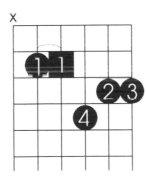
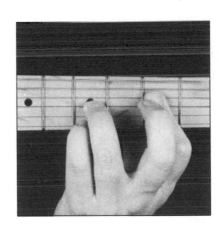
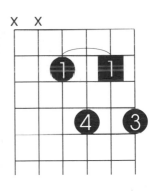

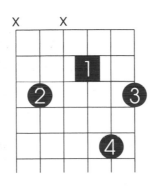

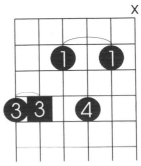

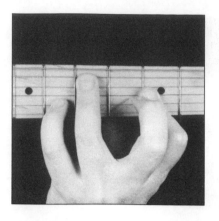
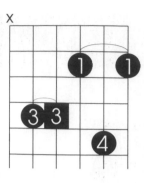

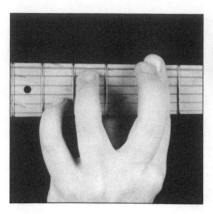
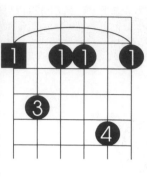

minor7♭5

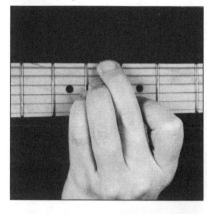
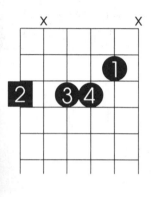

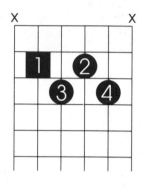

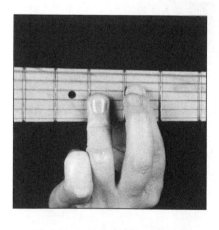
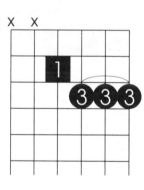

minor (major7)

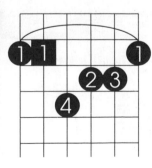

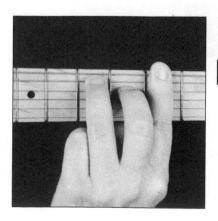
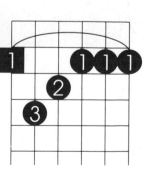

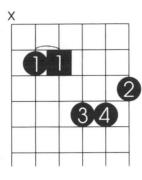

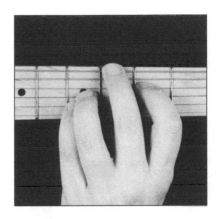
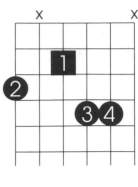

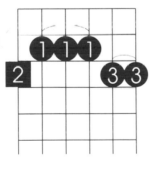
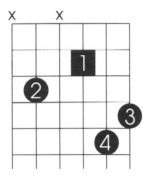

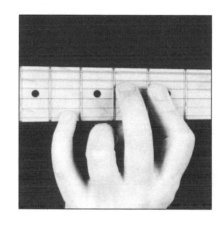
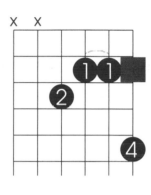

6/9

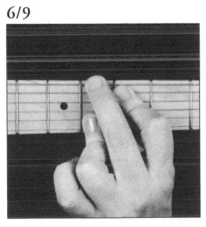
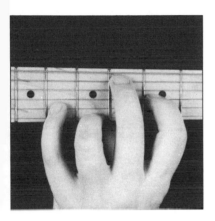

9

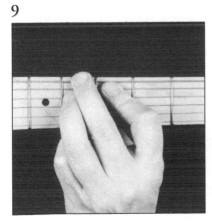
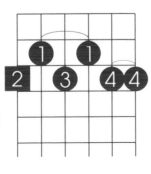

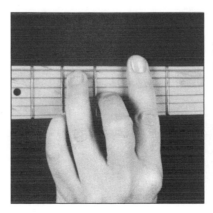
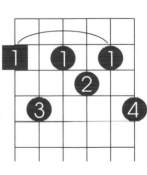

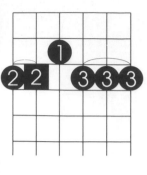
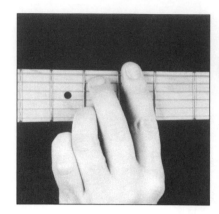
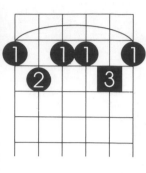

9sus4

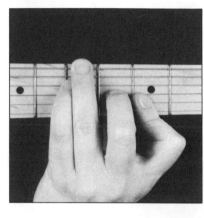
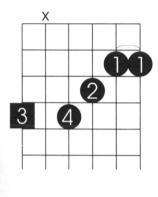

13

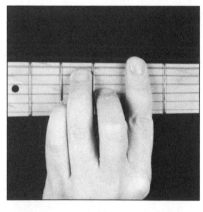
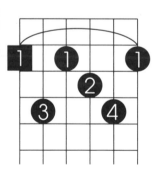
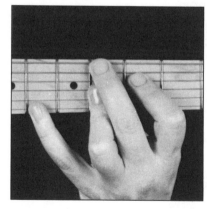
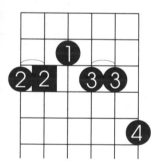

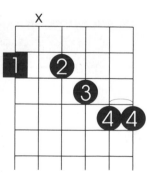

major9

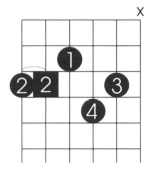

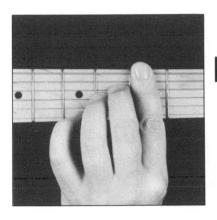

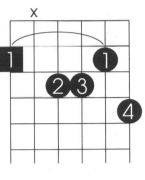

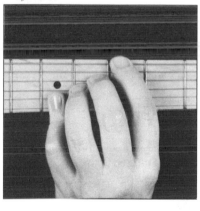

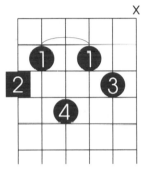

major13

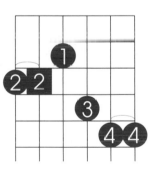

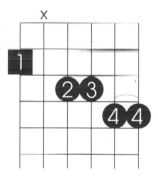

minor9

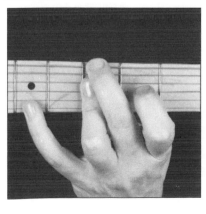

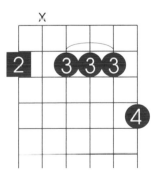

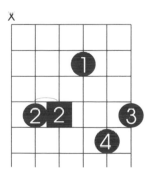

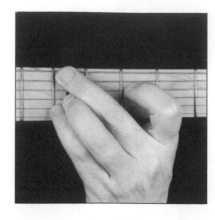

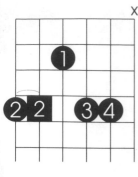

minor11

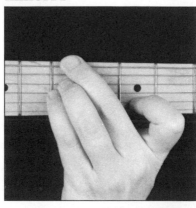

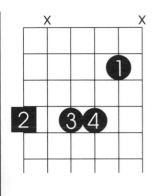

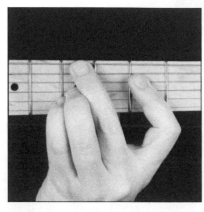

minor13

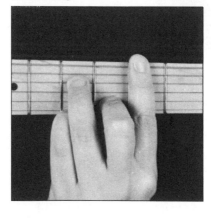

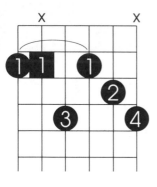

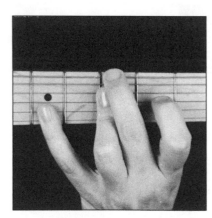

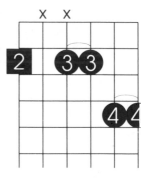

Alternate Chord Names

This chord encyclopedia uses a standard chord naming approach, but when playing from sheet music or using other music books, you will find alternative chord names or symbols. Below is a chart by which you can cross reference alternative names and symbols with the ones used in this book.

Chord Name	Alternate Name or Symbol
major	M; Maj
minor	m; min;
6	Maj6; M6
minor6	m6; min6
6/9	6(add9); Maj6(add9); M6(add9)
major7	M7; Maj7; △7
7	dominant seventh; dom
7♭5	7(♭5); 7(-5)
7♯5	+7; 7(+5); aug7
minor7	m7; min7; -7
minor(major7)	m(M7); min(Maj7); m(+7); -(M7); min(addM7)
∅7	½dim; ½dim7; m7(♭5); m7(-5)
°7	°; dim; dim7
9	7(add9)
9♭5	9(♭5); 9(-5)
9♯5	+9; 9(+5); aug9
major9	M9; △9; Maj7(add9); M7(add9)
minor9	m9; min9
7♭9	7(♭9); 7(add♭9); 7-9; -9
minor11	m11; min11
♯11	(+11); △(+11); M7(+11); △(♯11); M7(♯11)
13	7(add13); 7(add6)
major13	M13; △13; Maj7(add13); M7(add13); M7(add6)
minor13	m13; -13; min7(add13); m7(add13); -7(add13)
sus4	(sus4)